Other books in this series available in both hardcover
and paperback:

Lao Tsu/Tao Te Ching (1972)
A new translation by Gia-fu Feng and Jane English
Photography by Jane English
Calligraphy by Gia-fu Feng

Chuang Tsu/Inner Chapters (1974)
A new translation by Gia-fu Feng and Jane English
Photography by Jane English
Calligraphy by Gia-fu Feng

Hymns from the Rig-Veda (1975)
A new translation by Jean Le Mée
Photography by Ingbert Grüttner
Calligraphy by Jean Le Mée

The Dhammapada (1976)
A new rendering by Thomas Byrom
Photography by Sandra Weiner

THE BHAGAVAD GITA

THE BHA

TRANSLATION BY SHRI PUROHIT SWAMI   PHOTOGRAPHY BY CURT BRUCE

THE GOSPEL OF THE LORD SHRI KRISHNA

GAVAD GITA

ALFRED A. KNOPF   NEW YORK   1977

This is a Borzoi Book
Published by Alfred A. Knopf, Inc.

Photographs Copyright © 1977 by Curt Bruce

Library of Congress Cataloging in Publication Data

Mahābhārata. Bhagavadgītā. English.
    Bhagavad Gita: the gospel of the Lord Shri Krishna.

    I.   Purohit, Swami, 1882–1946   II.   Bruce, Curt.
III.   Title.
BL1130.A4P87   1977   294.5'924   77-74990
ISBN 0-394-40671-0

Manufactured in the United States of America

First Edition

CONTENTS

PREFACE

The Bhagavad Gita, the greatest devotional book of Hinduism, has long been recognized as one of the world's spiritual classics and a guide to all on the path of Truth. It is sometimes known as the Song of the Lord or the Gospel of the Lord Shri Krishna. According to Western scholarship, it was composed later than the Vedas and the Upanishads—probably between the fifth and second centuries before Christ. It is a fragment, part of the sixth book of the epic poem *The Mahabharata.*

The Mahabharata tells of the Pandavas, Prince Arjuna and his four brothers, growing up in north India at the court of their uncle, the blind King Dhritarashtra, after the death of their father, the previous ruler. There is always great rivalry between the Pandavas or sons of Pandu and the Kauravas, the one hundred sons of Dhritarashtra. Eventually the old king gives his nephews some land of their own but his eldest son, Duryodhana, defeats Yudhisthira, the eldest Pandava, by cheating at dice, and forces him and his brothers to surrender their land and go into exile for thirteen years. On their return, the old king is unable to persuade his son Duryodhana to restore their heritage and, in spite of efforts at reconciliation by Sanjaya, Dhritarashtra's charioteer; by Bheeshma, his wise counsellor; and even by the Lord Krishna himself, war cannot be averted. The rival hosts face each other on the field of Kurukshetra. It is at this point that *The Bhagavad Gita* begins.

When Prince Arjuna surveys the battlefield, he is overwhelmed with sorrow at the futility of war. The teachings of *The Bhagavad Gita* are spoken by the divine Lord Krishna, who is acting as the prince's charioteer. They are overheard by Sanjaya and reported back to King Dhritarashtra. When Krishna has finished speaking to Arjuna, the two armies engage. The battle lasts eighteen days and by the end of it nearly all the warriors on both sides are dead save Krishna and the five sons of Pandu.

This translation of *The Bhagavad Gita*, which was first published in London in 1935, has never before been readily available in the United States, yet it remains one of the simplest and loveliest of the many renderings that have been made.

THE BHAGAVAD GITA

ONE

THE DESPONDENCY OF ARJUNA

The King Dhritarashtra asked: "O Sanjaya! What happened on the sacred battlefield of Kurukshetra, when my people gathered against the Pandavas?"

Sanjaya replied: "The Prince Duryodhana, when he saw the army of the Pandavas paraded, approached his preceptor Guru Drona and spoke as follows:

Revered Father! Behold this mighty host of the Pandavas, paraded by the son of King Drupada, thy wise disciple.

In it are heroes and great bowmen; the equals in battle of Arjuna and Bheema, Yuyudhana, Virata and Drupada, great soldiers all;

Dhrishtaketu, Chekitan, the valiant King of Benares, Purujit, Kuntibhoja, Shaibya—a master over many;

Yudhamanyu, Uttamouja, Soubhadra and the sons of Droupadi, famous men.

Further, take note of all those captains who have ranged themselves on our side, O best of Spiritual Guides! The leaders of my army. I will name them for you.

You come first; then Bheeshma, Karna, Kripa, great soldiers; Ashwaththama, Vikarna and the son of Somadatta;

And many others, all ready to die for my sake, all armed, all skilled in war.

Yet our army seems the weaker, though commanded by Bheeshma; their army seems the stronger, though commanded by Bheema.

Therefore in the rank and file, let all stand firm in their posts, according to battalions; and all you generals about Bheeshma.

धृतराष्ट्र उवाच ।
धर्मक्षेत्रे कुरुक्षेत्रे समवेता युयुत्सवः ।
मामकाः पाण्डवाश्चैव किमकुर्वत संजय ॥ १
संजय उवाच ।
दृष्ट्वा तु पाण्डवानीकं व्यूढं दुर्योधनस्तदा ।
आचार्यमुपसंगम्य राजा वचनमब्रवीत् ॥ २
पश्यैतां पाण्डुपुत्राणामाचार्य महतीं चमूम् ।
व्यूढां द्रुपदपुत्रेण तव शिष्येण धीमता ॥ ३
अत्र शूरा महेष्वासा भीमार्जुनसमा युधि ।
युयुधानो विराटश्च द्रुपदश्च महारथः ॥ ४
धृष्टकेतुश्चेकितानः काशिराजश्च वीर्यवान् ।
पुरुजित्कुन्तिभोजश्च शैब्यश्च नरपुंगवः ॥ ५
युधामन्युश्च विक्रान्त उत्तमौजाश्च वीर्यवान् ।
सौभद्रो द्रौपदेयाश्च सर्व एव महारथाः ॥ ६
अस्माकं तु विशिष्टा ये तान्निबोध द्विजोत्तम ।
नायका मम सैन्यस्य संज्ञार्थं तान्ब्रवीमि ते ॥ ७
भवान्भीष्मश्च कर्णश्च कृपश्च समितिंजयः ।
अश्वत्थामा विकर्णश्च सौमदत्तिस्तथैव च ॥ ८
अन्ये च बहवः शूरा मदर्थे त्यक्तजीविताः ।
नानाशस्त्रप्रहरणाः सर्वे युद्धविशारदाः ॥ ९
अपर्याप्तं तदस्माकं बलं भीष्माभिरक्षितम् ।
पर्याप्तं त्विदमेतेषां बलं भीमाभिरक्षितम् ॥ १०
अयनेषु च सर्वेषु यथाभागमवस्थिताः ।
भीष्ममेवाभिरक्षन्तु भवन्तः सर्व एव हि ॥ ११

4

तस्य संजनयन्हर्षं कुरुवृद्धः पितामहः ।
सिंहनादं विनद्योच्चैः शङ्खं दध्मौ प्रतापवान् ॥ १२

ततः शङ्खाश्च भेर्यश्च पणवानकगोमुखाः ।
सहसैवाभ्यहन्यन्त स शब्दस्तुमुलोऽभवत् ॥ १३

ततः श्वेतैर्हयैर्युक्ते महति स्यन्दने स्थितौ ।
माधवः पाण्डवश्चैव दिव्यौ शङ्खौ प्रदध्मतुः ॥ १४

पाञ्चजन्यं हृषीकेशो देवदत्तं धनंजयः ।
पौण्ड्रं दध्मौ महाशङ्खं भीमकर्मा वृकोदरः ॥ १५

अनन्तविजयं राजा कुन्तीपुत्रो युधिष्ठिरः ।
नकुलः सहदेवश्च सुघोषमणिपुष्पकौ ॥ १६

काश्यश्च परमेष्वासः शिखण्डी च महारथः ।
धृष्टद्युम्नो विराटश्च सात्यकिश्चापराजितः ॥ १७

द्रुपदो द्रौपदेयाश्च सर्वशः पृथिवीपते ।
सौभद्रश्च महाबाहुः शङ्खान्दध्मुः पृथक्पृथक् ॥ १८

स घोषो धार्तराष्ट्राणां हृदयानि व्यदारयत् ।
नभश्च पृथिवीं चैव तुमुलो व्यनुनादयन् ॥ १९

अथ व्यवस्थितान्दृष्ट्वा धार्तराष्ट्रान्कपिध्वजः ।
प्रवृत्ते शस्त्रसंपाते धनुरुद्यम्य पाण्डवः ॥ २०

हृषीकेशं तदा वाक्यमिदमाह महीपते ।
सेनयोरुभयोर्मध्ये रथं स्थापय मेऽच्युत ॥ २१

यावदेतान्निरीक्षेऽहं योद्धुकामानवस्थितान् ।
कैर्मया सह योद्धव्यमस्मिन्रणसमुद्यमे ॥ २२

योत्स्यमानानवेक्षेऽहं य एतेऽत्र समागताः ।
धार्तराष्ट्रस्य दुर्बुद्धेर्युद्धे प्रियचिकीर्षवः ॥ २३

Then to enliven his spirits, the brave Grandfather Bheeshma, eldest of the Kuru-clan, blew his conch, till it sounded like a lion's roar.

And immediately all the conches and drums, the trumpets and horns, blared forth in tumultuous uproar.

Then seated in their spacious war chariot, yoked with white horses, Lord Shri Krishna and Arjuna sounded their divine shells.

Lord Shri Krishna blew His Panchajanya and Arjuna his Devadatta, brave Bheema his renowned shell, Poundra.

The King Dharmaraja, the son of Kunti, blew the Anantavijaya, Nakula and Sahadeo, the Sughosh and Manipushpaka, respectively.

And the Maharaja of Benares, the great archer, Shikhandi, the great soldier, Dhrishtadyumna, Virata and Satyaki, the invincible,

And O King! Drupada, the sons of Droupadi and Soubhadra, the great soldier, blew their conches.

The tumult rent the hearts of the sons of Dhritarashtra, and violently shook heaven and earth with its echo.

Then beholding the sons of Dhritarashtra, drawn up on the battlefield, ready to begin the fight, Arjuna, whose flag bore the Hanuman,

Raising his bow, spoke thus to the Lord Shri Krishna: O Infallible! Lord of the earth! Please draw up my chariot betwixt the two armies,

So that I may observe those who must fight on my side, those who must fight against me;

And gaze over this array of soldiers, eager to please the sinful son of Dhritarashtra."

एवमुक्तो हृषीकेशो गुडाकेशेन भारत ।
सेनयोरुभयोर्मध्ये स्थापयित्वा रथोत्तमम् ॥ २४
भीष्मद्रोणप्रमुखतः सर्वेषां च महीक्षिताम् ।
उवाच पार्थ पश्यैतान्समवेतान्कुरूनिति ॥ २५
तत्रापश्यत्स्थितान्पार्थः पितृनथ पितामहान् ।
आचार्यान्मातुलान्भ्रातृन्पुत्रान्पौत्रान्सखींस्तथा ॥ २६
श्वशुरान्सुहृदश्चैव सेनयोरुभयोरपि ।
तान्समीक्ष्य स कौन्तेयः सर्वान्बन्धूनवस्थितान् ॥ २७
कृपया परयाविष्टो विषीदन्निदमब्रवीत् ।
दृष्ट्वेमान्स्वजनान्कृष्ण युयुत्सून्समवस्थितान् ॥ २८
सीदन्ति मम गात्राणि मुखं च परिशुष्यति ।
वेपथुश्च शरीरे मे रोमहर्षश्च जायते ॥ २९
गाण्डीवं स्रंसते हस्तात्त्वक्चैव परिदह्यते ।
न च शक्नोम्यवस्थातुं भ्रमतीव च मे मनः ॥ ३०
निमित्तानि च पश्यामि विपरीतानि केशव ।
न च श्रेयोऽनुपश्यामि हत्वा स्वजनमाहवे ॥ ३१

Sanjaya said: "Having listened to the request of Arjuna, Lord Shri Krishna drew up His bright chariot exactly in the midst between the two armies,

Whither Bheeshma and Drona had led all the rulers of the earth, and spoke thus: O Arjuna! Behold these members of the family of Kuru assembled.

There Arjuna noticed fathers, grandfathers, uncles, cousins, sons, grandsons, teachers, friends;

Fathers-in-law and benefactors, arrayed on both sides. Arjuna then gazed at all those kinsmen before him.

And his heart melted with pity and sadly he spoke: O my Lord! When I see all these, my own people, thirsting for battle,

My limbs fail me and my throat is parched, my body trembles and my hair stands on end.

The bow Gandeeva slips from my hand, and my skin burns. I cannot keep quiet, for my mind is in a tumult.

The omens are adverse; what good can come from the slaughter of my people on this battlefield?

न काङ्क्षे विजयं कृष्ण न च राज्यं सुखानि च ।
किं नो राज्येन गोविन्द किं भोगैर्जीवितेन वा ॥ ३२
येषामर्थे काङ्क्षितं नो राज्यं भोगाः सुखानि च ।
त इमेऽवस्थिता युद्धे प्राणांस्त्यक्त्वा धनानि च ॥ ३३
आचार्याः पितरः पुत्रास्तथैव च पितामहाः ।
मातुलाः श्वशुराः पौत्राः स्यालाः संबन्धिनस्तथा ॥ ३४
एतान्न हन्तुमिच्छामि घ्नतोऽपि मधुसूदन ।
अपि त्रैलोक्यराज्यस्य हेतोः किं नु महीकृते ॥ ३५
निहत्य धार्तराष्ट्रान्नः का प्रीतिः स्याज्जनार्दन ।
पापमेवाश्रयेदस्मान्हत्वैतानाततायिनः ॥ ३६
तस्मान्नार्हा वयं हन्तुं धार्तराष्ट्रान्स्वबान्धवान् ।
स्वजनं हि कथं हत्वा सुखिनः स्याम माधव ॥ ३७
यद्यप्येते न पश्यन्ति लोभोपहतचेतसः ।
कुलक्षयकृतं दोषं मित्रद्रोहे च पातकम् ॥ ३८
कथं न ज्ञेयमस्माभिः पापादस्मान्निवर्तितुम् ।
कुलक्षयकृतं दोषं प्रपश्यद्भिर्जनार्दन ॥ ३९

Ah, my Lord! I crave not for victory, nor for kingdom, nor for any pleasure. What were a kingdom or happiness or life to me,

When those for whose sake I desire these things stand here about to sacrifice their property and their lives:

Teachers, fathers and grandfathers, sons and grandsons, uncles, fathers-in-law, brothers-in-law and other relatives.

I would not kill them, even for the three worlds; why then for this poor earth? It matters not if I myself am killed.

My Lord! What happiness can come from the death of these sons of Dhritarashtra? We shall sin if we kill these desperate men.

We are worthy of a nobler feat than to slaughter our relatives—the sons of Dhritarashtra; for, my Lord, how can we be happy if we kill our kinsmen?

Although these men, blinded by greed, see no guilt in destroying their kin, or fighting against their friends,

Should not we, whose eyes are open, who consider it to be wrong to annihilate our house, turn away from so great a crime?

The destruction of our kindred means the destruction of the traditions of our ancient lineage, and when these are lost, irreligion will overrun our homes.

When irreligion spreads, the women of the house begin to stray; when they lose their purity, adulteration of the stock follows.

Promiscuity ruins both the family and those who defile it; while the souls of our ancestors droop, through lack of the funeral cakes and ablutions.

By the destruction of our lineage and the pollution of blood, ancient class traditions and family purity alike perish.

The wise say, my Lord, that they are forever lost, whose ancient traditions are lost.

Alas, it is strange that we should be willing to kill our own countrymen and commit a great sin, in order to enjoy the pleasures of a kingdom.

If, on the contrary, the sons of Dhritarashtra, with weapons in their hands, should slay me, unarmed and unresisting, surely that would be better for my welfare!"

Sanjaya said: "Having spoken thus, in the midst of the armies, Arjuna sank on the seat of the chariot, casting away his bow and arrow, heartbroken with grief."

*Thus, in the Holy Book the Bhagavad Gita, one of the Upanishads, in the Science of the Supreme Spirit, in the Art of Self-Knowledge, in the colloquy between the Divine Lord Shri Krishna and the Prince Arjuna, stands the first chapter, entitled:
The Despondency of Arjuna.*

कुलक्षये प्रणश्यन्ति कुलधर्माः सनातनाः ।
धर्मे नष्टे कुलं कृत्स्नमधर्मोऽभिभवत्युत ॥ ४०
अधर्माभिभवात्कृष्ण प्रदुष्यन्ति कुलस्त्रियः ।
स्त्रीषु दुष्टासु वार्ष्णेय जायते वर्णसंकरः ॥ ४१
संकरो नरकायैव कुलघ्नानां कुलस्य च ।
पतन्ति पितरो ह्येषां लुप्तपिण्डोदकक्रियाः ॥ ४२
दोषैरेतैः कुलघ्नानां वर्णसंकरकारकैः ।
उत्साद्यन्ते जातिधर्माः कुलधर्माश्च शाश्वताः ॥ ४३
उत्सन्नकुलधर्माणां मनुष्याणां जनार्दन ।
नरके नियतं वासो भवतीत्यनुशुश्रुम ॥ ४४
अहो बत महत्पापं कर्तुं व्यवसिता वयम् ।
यद्राज्यसुखलोभेन हन्तुं स्वजनमुद्यताः ॥ ४५
यदि मामप्रतीकारमशस्त्रं शस्त्रपाणयः ।
धार्तराष्ट्रा रणे हन्युस्तन्मे क्षेमतरं भवेत् ॥ ४६
एवमुक्त्वार्जुनः संख्ये रथोपस्थ उपाविशत् ।
विसृज्य सशरं चापं शोकसंविग्नमानसः ॥ ४७

इति श्रीमद्भगवद्गीतासु प्रथमोऽध्यायः ॥ १ ॥

TWO

·2·

THE PHILOSOPHY OF
DISCRIMINATION

Sanjaya then told how the Lord Shri Krishna, seeing Arjuna over-whelmed with compassion, his eyes dimmed with flowing tears and full of despondency, consoled him:

"*The Lord said:* My beloved friend! Why yield, just on the eve of battle, to this weakness which does no credit to those who call themselves Aryans, and only brings them infamy and bars against them the gates of heaven?

O Arjuna! Why give way to unmanliness? O thou who art the terror of thine enemies! Shake off such shameful effeminacy, make ready to act!

Arjuna argued: My Lord! How can I, when the battle rages, send an arrow through Bheeshma and Drona, who should receive my reverence?

Rather would I content myself with a beggar's crust than kill these teachers of mine, these precious noble souls! To slay these masters who are my benefactors would be to stain the sweetness of life's pleasure with their blood.

Nor can I say whether it were better that they conquer me or for me to conquer them, since I would no longer care to live if I killed these sons of Dhritarashtra, now preparing for fight.

My heart is oppressed with pity; and my mind confused as to what my duty is. Therefore, my Lord, tell me what is best for my spiritual welfare, for I am Thy disciple. Please direct me, I pray.

For should I attain the monarchy of the visible world, or over the invisible world, it would not drive away the anguish which is now paralysing my senses."

संजय उवाच ।
तं तथा कृपयाविष्टमश्रुपूर्णाकुलेक्षणम् ।
विषीदन्तमिदं वाक्यमुवाच मधुसूदनः ॥ १
श्रीभगवानुवाच ।
कुतस्त्वा कश्मलमिदं विषमे समुपस्थितम् ।
अनार्यजुष्टमस्वर्ग्यमकीर्तिकरमर्जुन ॥ २
क्लैब्यं मा स्म गमः पार्थ नैतत्त्वय्युपपद्यते ।
क्षुद्रं हृदयदौर्बल्यं त्यक्त्वोत्तिष्ठ परंतप ॥ ३
अर्जुन उवाच ।
कथं भीष्ममहं संख्ये द्रोणं च मधुसूदन ।
इषुभिः प्रतियोत्स्यामि पूजार्हावरिसूदन ॥ ४
गुरूनहत्वा हि महानुभावा-
ञ्श्रेयो भोक्तुं भैक्ष्यमपीह लोके ।
हत्वार्थकामांस्तु गुरूनिहैव
भुञ्जीय भोगान्रुधिरप्रदिग्धान् ॥ ५
न चैतद्विद्मः कतरन्नो गरीयो
यद्वा जयेम यदि वा नो जयेयुः ।
यानेव हत्वा न जिजीविषाम-
स्तेऽवस्थिताः प्रमुखे धार्तराष्ट्राः ॥ ६
कार्पण्यदोषोपहतस्वभावः
पृच्छामि त्वां धर्मसंमूढचेताः ।
यच्छ्रेयः स्यान्निश्चितं ब्रूहि तन्मे
शिष्यस्तेऽहं शाधि मां त्वां प्रपन्नम् ॥ ७
न हि प्रपश्यामि ममापनुद्या-
द्यच्छोकमुच्छोषणमिन्द्रियाणाम् ।
अवाप्य भूमावसपत्नमृद्धं
राज्यं सुराणामपि चाधिपत्यम् ॥ ८

संजय उवाच ।

एवमुक्त्वा हृषीकेशं गुडाकेशः परंतप ।
न योत्स्य इति गोविन्दमुक्त्वा तूष्णीं बभूव ह ॥ ९

तमुवाच हृषीकेशः प्रहसन्निव भारत ।
सेनयोरुभयोर्मध्ये विषीदन्तमिदं वचः ॥ १०

श्रीभगवानुवाच ।

अशोच्यानन्वयाशोचस्त्वं प्रज्ञावादांश्च भाषसे ।
गतासूनगतासूंश्च नानुशोचन्ति पण्डिताः ॥ ११

न त्वेवाहं जातु नासं न त्वं नेमे जनाधिपाः ।
न चैव न भविष्यामः सर्वे वयमतः परम् ॥ १२

देहिनोऽस्मिन्यथा देहे कौमारं यौवनं जरा ।
तथा देहान्तरप्राप्तिर्धीरस्तत्र न मुह्यति ॥ १३

मात्रास्पर्शास्तु कौन्तेय शीतोष्णसुखदुःखदाः ।
आगमापायिनोऽनित्यास्तांस्तितिक्षस्व भारत ॥ १४

यं हि न व्यथयन्त्येते पुरुषं पुरुषर्षभ ।
समदुःखसुखं धीरं सोऽमृतत्वाय कल्पते ॥ १५

नासतो विद्यते भावो नाभावो विद्यते सतः ।
उभयोरपि दृष्टोऽन्तस्त्वनयोस्तत्त्वदर्शिभिः ॥ १६

अविनाशि तु तद्विद्धि येन सर्वमिदं ततम् ।
विनाशमव्ययस्यास्य न कश्चित्कर्तुमर्हति ॥ १७

अन्तवन्त इमे देहा नित्यस्योक्ताः शरीरिणः ।
अनाशिनोऽप्रमेयस्य तस्माद्युध्यस्व भारत ॥ १८

Sanjaya continued: "Arjuna, the conqueror of all enemies, then told the Lord of All-Hearts that he would not fight, and became silent, O King!

Thereupon the Lord, with a gracious smile, addressed him who was so much depressed in the midst between the two armies.

Lord Shri Krishna said: Why grieve for those for whom no grief is due, and yet profess wisdom? The wise grieve neither for the dead nor for the living.

There was never a time when I was not, nor thou, nor these princes were not; there will never be a time when we shall cease to be.

As the soul experiences in this body infancy, youth and old age, so finally it passes into another. The wise have no delusion about this.

Those external relations which bring cold and heat, pain and happiness, they come and go; they are not permanent. Endure them bravely, O Prince!

The hero whose soul is unmoved by circumstance, who accepts pleasure and pain with equanimity, only he is fit for immortality.

That which is not, shall never be; that which is, shall never cease to be. To the wise, these truths are self-evident.

The Spirit, which pervades all that we see, is imperishable. Nothing can destroy the Spirit.

The material bodies which this Eternal, Indestructible, Immeasurable Spirit inhabits are all finite. Therefore fight, O Valiant Man!

य एनं वेत्ति हन्तारं यश्चैनं मन्यते हतम् ।
उभौ तौ न विजानीतो नायं हन्ति न हन्यते ॥ १९

न जायते म्रियते वा कदाचि-
      न्नायं भूत्वा भविता वा न भूयः ।
अजो नित्यः शाश्वतोऽयं पुराणो
      न हन्यते हन्यमाने शरीरे ॥ २०

वेदाविनाशिनं नित्यं य एनमजमव्ययम् ।
कथं स पुरुषः पार्थ कं घातयति हन्ति कम् ॥ २१

वासांसि जीर्णानि यथा विहाय
      नवानि गृह्णाति नरोऽपराणि ।
तथा शरीराणि विहाय जीर्णा-
      न्यन्यानि संयाति नवानि देही ॥ २२

नैनं छिन्दन्ति शस्त्राणि नैनं दहति पावकः ।
न चैनं क्लेदयन्त्यापो न शोषयति मारुतः ॥ २३

अच्छेद्योऽयमदाह्योऽयमक्लेद्योऽशोष्य एव च ।
नित्यः सर्वगतः स्थाणुरचलोऽयं सनातनः ॥ २४

अव्यक्तोऽयमचिन्त्योऽयमविकार्योऽयमुच्यते ।
तस्मादेवं विदित्वैनं नानुशोचितुमर्हसि ॥ २५

अथ चैनं नित्यजातं नित्यं वा मन्यसे मृतम् च ।
तथापि त्वं महाबाहो नैनं शोचितुमर्हसि ॥ २६

जातस्य हि ध्रुवो मृत्युर्ध्रुवं जन्म मृतस्य च ।
तस्मादपरिहार्येऽर्थे न त्वं शोचितुमर्हसि ॥ २७

He who thinks that the Spirit kills, and he who thinks of It as killed, are both ignorant. The spirit kills not, nor is It killed.

It was not born; It will never die, nor once having been, can It ever cease to be. Unborn, Eternal, Ever-enduring, yet Most Ancient, the Spirit dies not when the body is dead.

He who knows the Spirit as Indestructible, Immortal, Unborn, Always-the-Same, how should he kill or cause to be killed?

As a man discards his threadbare robes and puts on new, so the Spirit throws off Its worn-out bodies and takes fresh ones.

Weapons cleave It not, fire burns It not, water drenches It not, and wind dries It not.

It is impenetrable; It can be neither drowned nor scorched nor dried. It is Eternal, All-pervading, Unchanging, Immovable and Most Ancient.

It is named the Unmanifest, the Unthinkable, the Immutable. Wherefore, knowing the Spirit as such, thou hast no cause to grieve.

Even if thou thinkest of It as constantly being born, constantly dying, even then, O Mighty Man, thou still hast no cause to grieve.

For death is as sure for that which is born, as birth is for that which is dead. Therefore grieve not for what is inevitable.

The end and beginning of beings are unknown. We see only the intervening formations. Then what cause is there for grief?

One hears of the Spirit with surprise, another thinks It marvellous, the third listens without comprehending. Thus, though many are told about It, scarcely is there one who knows It.

Be not anxious about these armies. The Spirit in man is imperishable.

Thou must look at thy duty. Nothing can be more welcome to a soldier than a righteous war. Therefore to waver in thy resolve is unworthy, O Arjuna!

Blessed are the soldiers who find their opportunity. This opportunity has opened for thee the gates of heaven.

Refuse to fight in this righteous cause, and thou wilt be a traitor, lost to fame, incurring only sin.

Men will talk forever of thy disgrace; and to the noble, dishonour is worse than death.

Great generals will think that thou hast fled from the battlefield through cowardice; though once honoured thou wilt seem despicable.

Thine enemies will spread scandal and mock at thy courage. Can anything be more humiliating?

If killed, thou shalt attain Heaven; if victorious, enjoy the kingdom of earth. Therefore arise, O son of Kunti, and fight!

Look upon pleasure and pain, victory and defeat, with an equal eye. Make ready for the combat, and thou shalt commit no sin.

अव्यक्तादीनि भूतानि व्यक्तमध्यानि भारत ।
अव्यक्तनिधनान्येव तत्र का परिदेवना ॥ २८

आश्चर्यवत्पश्यति कश्चिदेन-
	माश्चर्यवद्वदति तथैव चान्यः ।
आश्चर्यवच्चैनमन्यः शृणोति
	श्रुत्वाप्येनं वेद न चैव कश्चित् ॥ २९

देही नित्यमवध्योऽयं देहे सर्वस्य भारत ।
तस्मात्सर्वाणि भूतानि न त्वं शोचितुमर्हसि ॥ ३०

स्वधर्ममपि चावेक्ष्य न विकम्पितुमर्हसि ।
धर्म्याद्धि युद्धाच्छ्रेयोऽन्यत्क्षत्रियस्य न विद्यते ॥ ३१

यदृच्छया चोपपन्नं स्वर्गद्वारमपावृतम् ।
सुखिनः क्षत्रियाः पार्थ लभन्ते युद्धमीदृशम् ॥ ३२

अथ चेत्त्वमिमं धर्म्यं सग्राम न करिष्यासि ।
ततः स्वधर्मं कीर्तिं च हित्वा पापमवाप्स्यसि ॥ ३३

अकीर्तिं चापि भूतानि कथयिष्यन्ति तेऽव्ययाम् ।
संभावितस्य चाकीर्तिर्मरणादतिरिच्यते ॥ ३४

भयाद्रणादुपरतं मंस्यन्ते त्वां महारथाः ।
येषां च त्वं बहुमतो भूत्वा यास्यसि लाघवम् ॥ ३५

अवाच्यवादांश्च बहून्वदिष्यन्ति तवाहिताः ।
निन्दन्तस्तव सामर्थ्यं ततो दुःखतरं नु किम् ॥ ३६

हतो वा प्राप्स्यसि स्वर्गं जित्वा वा भोक्ष्यसे महीम् ।
तस्मादुत्तिष्ठ कौन्तेय युद्धाय कृतनिश्चयः ॥ ३७

सुखदुःखे समे कृत्वा लाभालाभौ जयाजयौ ।
ततो युद्धाय युज्यस्व नैवं पापमवाप्स्यसि ॥ ३८

I have told thee the philosophy of Knowledge. Now listen and I will explain the philosophy of Action, by means of which, O Arjuna, thou shalt break through the bondage of all action.

On this Path, endeavour is never wasted, nor can it ever be repressed. Even a very little of its practice protects one from great danger.

By its means, the straying intellect becomes steadied in the contemplation of one object only; whereas the minds of the irresolute stray into bypaths innumerable.

Only the ignorant speak in figurative language. It is they who extol the letter of the scriptures, saying, 'There is nothing deeper than this.'

Consulting only their desires, they construct their own heaven, devising arduous and complex rites to secure their own pleasure and their own power; and the only result is rebirth.

While their minds are absorbed with ideas of power and personal enjoyment, they cannot concentrate their discrimination on one point.

एषा तेऽभिहिता सांख्ये बुद्धियोंगे त्विमां शृणु ।
बुद्ध्या युक्तो यया पार्थ कर्मबन्धं प्रहास्यसि ॥ ३९
नेहाभिक्रमनाशोऽस्ति प्रत्यवायो न विद्यते ।
खल्पमप्यस्य धर्मस्य त्रायते महतो भयात् ॥ ४०
व्यवसायात्मिका बुद्धिरेकेह कुरुनन्दन ।
बहुशाखा ह्यनन्ताश्च बुद्धयोऽव्यवसायिनाम् ॥ ४१
यामिमां पुष्पितां वाचं प्रवदन्त्यविपश्चितः ।
वेदवादरताः पार्थ नान्यदस्तीति वादिनः ॥ ४२
कामात्मानः स्वर्गपरा जन्मकर्मफलप्रदाम् ।
क्रियाविशेषबहुलां भोगैश्वर्यगतिं प्रति ॥ ४३
भोगैश्वर्यप्रसक्तानां तयापहृतचेतसाम् ।
व्यवसायात्मिका बुद्धिः समाधौ न विधीयते ॥ ४४

त्रैगुण्यविषया वेदा निस्त्रैगुण्यो भवार्जुन ।
निर्द्वन्द्वो नित्यसत्त्वस्थो निर्योगक्षेम आत्मवान् ॥ ४५
यावानर्थ उदपाने सर्वतःसंप्लुतोदके ।
तावान्सर्वेषु वेदेषु ब्राह्मणस्य विजानतः ॥ ४६
कर्मण्येवाधिकारस्ते मा फलेषु कदाचन ।
मा कर्मफलहेतुर्भूर्मा ते सङ्गोऽस्त्वकर्मणि ॥ ४७
योगस्थः कुरु कर्माणि सङ्गं त्यक्त्वा धनंजय ।
सिद्ध्यसिद्ध्योः समो भूत्वा समत्वं योग उच्यते ॥ ४८
दूरेण ह्यवरं कर्म बुद्धियोगाद्धनंजय ।
बुद्धौ शरणमन्विच्छ कृपणाः फलहेतवः ॥ ४९
बुद्धियुक्तो जहातीह उभे सुकृतदुष्कृते ।
तस्माद्योगाय युज्यस्व योगः कर्मसु कौशलम् ॥ ५०
कर्मजं बुद्धियुक्ता हि फलं त्यक्त्वा मनीषिणः ।
जन्मबन्धविनिर्मुक्ताः पदं गच्छन्त्यनामयम् ॥ ५१
यदा ते मोहकलिलं बुद्धिर्व्यतितरिष्यति ।
तदा गन्तासि निर्वेदं श्रोतव्यस्य श्रुतस्य च ॥ ५२
श्रुतिविप्रतिपन्ना ते यदा स्थास्यति निश्चला ।
समाधावचला बुद्धिस्तदा योगमवाप्स्यसि ॥ ५३

The Vedic Scriptures tell of the three constituents of life—the Qualities. Rise above all of them, O Arjuna, above all the pairs of opposing sensations; be steady in truth, free from worldly anxieties and centred in the Self.

As a man can drink water from any side of a full tank, so the skilled theologian can wrest from any scripture that which will serve his purpose.

But thou hast only the right to work, but none to the fruit thereof. Let not then the fruit of thy action be thy motive; nor yet be thou enamoured of inaction.

Perform all thy actions with mind concentrated on the Divine, renouncing attachment and looking upon success and failure with an equal eye. Spirituality implies equanimity.

Physical action is far inferior to an intellect concentrated on the Divine. Have recourse then to the Pure Intelligence. It is only the petty-minded who work for reward.

When a man attains to Pure Reason, he renounces in this world the results of good and evil alike. Cling thou to Right Action. Spirituality is the real art of living.

The sages guided by Pure Intellect renounce the fruit of action; and, freed from the chains of rebirth, they reach the highest bliss.

When thy reason has crossed the entanglements of illusion, then shalt thou become indifferent both to the philosophies thou hast heard and to those thou mayest yet hear.

When the intellect, bewildered by the multiplicity of holy scripts, stands unperturbed in blissful contemplation of the Infinite, then hast thou attained Spirituality.

Arjuna asked: My Lord! How can we recognise the saint who has attained Pure Intellect, who has reached this state of Bliss, and whose mind is steady? How does he talk, how does he live, and how does he act?

Lord Shri Krishna replied: When a man has given up the desires of his heart and is satisfied with the Self alone, be sure that he has reached the highest state.

The sage, whose mind is unruffled in suffering, whose desire is not roused by enjoyment, who is without attachment, anger or fear—take him to be one who stands at that lofty level.

He who wherever he goes is attached to no person and to no place by ties of flesh; who accepts good and evil alike, neither welcoming the one nor shrinking from the other—take him to be one who is merged in the Infinite.

He who can withdraw his senses from the attraction of their objects, as the tortoise draws his limbs within his shell—take it that such a one has attained Perfection.

The objects of sense turn from him who is abstemious. Even the relish for them is lost in him who has seen the Truth.

अर्जुन उवाच ।
स्थितप्रज्ञस्य का भाषा समाधिस्थस्य केशव ।
स्थितधीः किं प्रभाषेत किमासीत व्रजेत किम् ॥ ५४
    श्रीभगवानुवाच ।
प्रजहाति यदा कामान्सर्वान्पार्थ मनोगतान् ।
आत्मन्येवात्मना तुष्टः स्थितप्रज्ञस्तदोच्यते ॥ ५५
दुःखेष्वनुद्विग्नमनाः सुखेषु विगतस्पृहः ।
वीतरागभयक्रोधः स्थितधीर्मुनिरुच्यते ॥ ५६
यः सर्वत्रानभिस्नेहस्तत्तत्प्राप्य शुभाशुभम् ।
नाभिनन्दति न द्वेष्टि तस्य प्रज्ञा प्रतिष्ठिता ॥ ५७
यदा संहरते चायं कूर्मोऽङ्गानीव सर्वशः ।
इन्द्रियाणीन्द्रियार्थेभ्यस्तस्य प्रज्ञा प्रतिष्ठिता ॥ ५८
विषया विनिवर्तन्ते निराहारस्य देहिनः ।
रसवर्जं रसोऽप्यस्य परं दृष्ट्वा निवर्तते ॥ ५९

O Arjuna! The mind of him, who is trying to conquer it, is forcibly carried away in spite of his efforts, by his tumultuous senses.

Restraining them all, let him meditate steadfastly on Me; for who thus conquers his senses achieves perfection.

When a man dwells on the objects of sense, he creates an attraction for them; attraction develops into desire, and desire breeds anger.

Anger induces delusion; delusion, loss of memory; through loss of memory, reason is shattered; and loss of reason leads to destruction.

But the self-controlled soul, who moves amongst sense objects, free from either attachment or repulsion, he wins eternal Peace.

Having attained Peace, he becomes free from misery; for when the mind gains peace, right discrimination follows.

Right discrimination is not for him who cannot concentrate. Without concentration, there cannot be meditation; he who cannot meditate must not expect peace; and without peace, how can anyone expect happiness?

As a ship at sea is tossed by the tempest, so the reason is carried away by the mind when preyed upon by the straying senses.

Therefore, O Mighty-in-Arms, he who keeps his senses detached from their objects—take it that his reason is purified.

यततो ह्यपि कौन्तेय पुरुषस्य विपश्चितः ।
इन्द्रियाणि प्रमाथीनि हरन्ति प्रसभं मनः ॥ ६० ॥
तानि सर्वाणि संयम्य युक्त आसीत मत्परः ।
वशे हि यस्येन्द्रियाणि तस्य प्रज्ञा प्रतिष्ठिता ॥ ६१ ॥
ध्यायतो विषयान्पुंसः सङ्गस्तेषूपजायते ।
सङ्गात्संजायते कामः कामात्क्रोधोऽभिजायते ॥ ६२ ॥
क्रोधाद्भवति संमोहः संमोहात्स्मृतिविभ्रमः ।
स्मृतिभ्रंशाद्बुद्धिनाशो बुद्धिनाशात्प्रणश्यति ॥ ६३ ॥
रागद्वेषवियुक्तैस्तु विषयानिन्द्रियैश्चरन् ।
आत्मवश्यैर्विधेयात्मा प्रसादमधिगच्छति ॥ ६४ ॥
प्रसादे सर्वदुःखानां हानिरस्योपजायते ।
प्रसन्नचेतसो ह्याशु बुद्धिः पर्यवतिष्ठते ॥ ६५ ॥
नास्ति बुद्धिरयुक्तस्य न चायुक्तस्य भावना ।
न चाभावयतः शान्तिरशान्तस्य कुतः सुखम् ॥ ६६ ॥
इन्द्रियाणां हि चरतां यन्मनोऽनुविधीयते ।
तदस्य हरति प्रज्ञां वायुर्नावमिवाम्भसि ॥ ६७ ॥
तस्माद्यस्य महाबाहो निगृहीतानि सर्वशः ।
इन्द्रियाणीन्द्रियार्थेभ्यस्तस्य प्रज्ञा प्रतिष्ठिता ॥ ६८ ॥

या निशा सर्वभूतानां तस्यां जागर्ति संयमी ।
यस्यां जाग्रति भूतानि सा निशा पश्यतो मुनेः ॥ ६९
आपूर्यमाणमचलप्रतिष्ठं
    समुद्रमापः प्रविशन्ति यद्वत् ।
तद्वत्कामा यं प्रविशन्ति सर्वे
    स शान्तिमाप्नोति न कामकामी ॥ ७०
विहाय कामान्यः सर्वान्पुमांश्चरति निःस्पृहः ।
निर्ममो निरहंकारः स शान्तिमधिगच्छति ॥ ७१
एषा ब्राह्मी स्थितिः पार्थ नैनां प्राप्य विमुह्यति ।
स्थित्वास्यामन्तकालेऽपि ब्रह्मनिर्वाणमृच्छति ॥ ७२

इति श्रीमद्भगवद्गीतासु द्वितीयोऽध्यायः ॥ २ ॥

The saint is awake when the world sleeps, and he ignores that for which the world lives.

He attains Peace, into whom desires flow as rivers into the ocean, which though brimming with water remains ever the same; not he whom desire carries away.

He attains Peace who, giving up desire, moves through the world without aspiration, possessing nothing which he can call his own, and free from pride.

O Arjuna! This is the state of the Self, the Supreme Spirit, to which if a man once attain, it shall never be taken from him. Even at the time of leaving the body, he will remain firmly enthroned there, and will become one with the Eternal."

Thus, in the Holy Book the Bhagavad Gita, one of the Upanishads, in the Science of the Supreme Spirit, in the Art of Self-Knowledge, in the colloquy between the Divine Lord Shri Krishna and the Prince Arjuna, stands the second chapter, entitled: The Philosophy of Discrimination.

THREE
३
KARMA-YOGA
—THE PATH OF ACTION

अर्जुन उवाच ।

ज्यायसी चेत्कर्मणस्ते मता बुद्धिर्जनार्दन ।
तत्किं कर्मणि घोरे मां नियोजयसि केशव ॥ १

व्यामिश्रेणेव वाक्येन बुद्धिं मोहयसीव मे ।
तदेकं वद निश्चित्य येन श्रेयोऽहमाप्नुयाम् ॥ २

श्रीभगवानुवाच ।

लोकेऽस्मिन्द्विविधा निष्ठा पुरा प्रोक्ता मयानघ ।
ज्ञानयोगेन सांख्यानां कर्मयोगेन योगिनाम् ॥ ३

न कर्मणामनारम्भान्नैष्कर्म्यं पुरुषोऽश्नुते ।
न च संन्यसनादेव सिद्धिं समधिगच्छति ॥ ४

न हि कश्चित्क्षणमपि जातु तिष्ठत्यकर्मकृत् ।
कार्यते ह्यवशः कर्म सर्वः प्रकृतिजैर्गुणैः ॥ ५

कर्मेन्द्रियाणि संयम्य य आस्ते मनसा स्मरन् ।
इन्द्रियार्थान्विमूढात्मा मिथ्याचारः स उच्यते ॥ ६

यस्त्विन्द्रियाणि मनसा नियम्यारभतेऽर्जुन ।
कर्मेन्द्रियैः कर्मयोगमसक्तः स विशिष्यते ॥ ७

नियतं कुरु कर्म त्वं कर्म ज्यायो ह्यकर्मणः ।
शरीरयात्रापि च ते न प्रसिध्येदकर्मणः ॥ ८

यज्ञार्थात्कर्मणोऽन्यत्र लोकोऽयं कर्मबन्धनः ।
तदर्थं कर्म कौन्तेय मुक्तसङ्गः समाचर ॥ ९

"Arjuna questioned: My Lord! If wisdom is above action, why dost Thou advise me to engage in this terrible fight?

Thy language perplexes me and confuses my reason. Therefore please tell me the only way by which I may, without doubt, secure my spiritual welfare.

Lord Shri Krishna replied: In this world, as I have said, there is a twofold path, O Sinless One! There is the Path of Wisdom for those who meditate, and the Path of Action for those who work.

No man can attain freedom from activity by refraining from action; nor can he reach perfection by merely refusing to act.

He cannot even for a moment remain really inactive, for the Qualities of Nature will compel him to act whether he will or no.

He who remains motionless, refusing to act, but all the while brooding over sensuous objects, that deluded soul is simply a hypocrite.

But, O Arjuna! All honour to him whose mind controls his senses, for he is thereby beginning to practise Karma-Yoga, the Path of Right Action, keeping himself always unattached.

Do thy duty as prescribed, for action for duty's sake is superior to inaction. Even the maintenance of the body would be impossible if man remained inactive.

In this world people are fettered by action, unless it is performed as a sacrifice. Therefore, O Arjuna, let thy acts be done without attachment, as sacrifice only.

सहयज्ञाः प्रजाः सृष्ट्वा पुरोवाच प्रजापतिः ।
अनेन प्रसविष्यध्वमेष वोऽस्त्विष्टकामधुक् ॥ १० ॥

देवान्भावयतानेन ते देवा भावयन्तु वः ।
परस्परं भावयन्तः श्रेयः परमवाप्स्यथ ॥ ११ ॥

इष्टान्भोगान्हि वो देवा दास्यन्ते यज्ञभाविताः ।
तैर्दत्तानप्रदायैभ्यो यो भुङ्क्ते स्तेन एव सः ॥ १२ ॥

यज्ञशिष्टाशिनः सन्तो मुच्यन्ते सर्वकिल्बिषैः ।
भुञ्जते ते त्वघं पापा ये पचन्त्यात्मकारणात् ॥ १३ ॥

अन्नाद्भवन्ति भूतानि पर्जन्यादन्नसंभवः ।
यज्ञाद्भवति पर्जन्यो यज्ञः कर्मसमुद्भवः ॥ १४ ॥

कर्म ब्रह्मोद्भवं विद्धि ब्रह्माक्षरसमुद्भवम् ।
तस्मात्सर्वगतं ब्रह्म नित्यं यज्ञे प्रतिष्ठितम् ॥ १५ ॥

एवं प्रवर्तितं चक्रं नानुवर्तयतीह यः ।
अघायुरिन्द्रियारामो मोघं पार्थ स जीवति ॥ १६ ॥

यस्त्वात्मरतिरेव स्यादात्मतृप्तश्च मानवः ।
आत्मन्येव च संतुष्टस्तस्य कार्यं न विद्यते ॥ १७ ॥

नैव तस्य कृतेनार्थो नाकृतेनेह कश्चन ।
न चास्य सर्वभूतेषु कश्चिदर्थव्यपाश्रयः ॥ १८ ॥

तस्मादसक्तः सततं कार्यं कर्म समाचर ।
असक्तो ह्याचरन्कर्म परमाप्नोति पूरुषः ॥ १९ ॥

In the beginning, when God created all beings by the sacrifice of Himself, He said unto them: 'Through sacrifice you can procreate, and it shall satisfy all your desires.

Worship the Powers of Nature thereby, and let them nourish you in return; thus supporting each other, you shall attain your highest welfare.

For, fed on sacrifice, Nature will give you all the enjoyment you can desire. But he who enjoys what she gives without returning is, indeed, a robber.'

The sages who enjoy the food that remains after the sacrifice is made are freed from all sin; but the selfish who spread their feast only for themselves feed on sin only.

All creatures are the product of food, food is the product of rain, rain comes by sacrifice, and sacrifice is the noblest form of action.

All action originates in the Supreme Spirit, which is Imperishable, and in sacrificial action the all-pervading Spirit is consciously present.

Thus he who does not help the revolving wheel of sacrifice, but instead leads a sinful life, rejoicing in the gratification of his senses, O Arjuna, he breathes in vain.

On the other hand, the soul who meditates on the Self is content to serve the Self and rests satisfied within the Self; there remains nothing more for him to accomplish.

He has nothing to gain by the performance or non-performance of action. His welfare depends not on any contribution that an earthly creature can make.

Therefore do thy duty perfectly, without care for the results, for he who does his duty disinterestedly attains the Supreme.

King Janaka and others attained perfection through action alone. Even for the sake of enlightening the world, it is thy duty to act;

For whatever a great man does, others imitate. People conform to the standard which he has set.

There is nothing in this universe, O Arjuna, that I am compelled to do, nor anything for Me to attain; yet I am persistently active.

For were I not to act without ceasing, O Prince, people would be glad to do likewise.

And if I were to refrain from action, the human race would be ruined; I should lead the world to chaos, and destruction would follow.

As the ignorant act, because of their fondness for action, so should the wise act without such attachment, fixing their eyes, O Arjuna, only on the welfare of the world.

But a wise man should not perturb the minds of the ignorant, who are attached to action; let him perform his own actions in the right spirit, with concentration on Me, thus inspiring all to do the same.

Action is the product of the Qualities inherent in Nature. It is only the ignorant man who, misled by personal egotism, says: 'I am the doer.'

कर्मणैव हि संसिद्धिमास्थिता जनकादयः ।
लोकसंग्रहमेवापि संपश्यन्कर्तुमर्हसि ॥ २०
यद्यदाचरति श्रेष्ठस्तत्तदेवेतरो जनः ।
स यत्प्रमाणं कुरुते लोकस्तदनुवर्तते ॥ २१
न मे पार्थास्ति कर्तव्यं त्रिषु लोकेषु किंचन ।
नानवाप्तमवाप्तव्यं वर्त एव च कर्मणि ॥ २२
यदि ह्यहं न वर्तेयं जातु कर्मण्यतन्द्रितः ।
मम वर्त्मानुवर्तन्ते मनुष्याः पार्थ सर्वशः ॥ २३
उत्सीदेयुरिमे लोका न कुर्यां कर्म चेदहम् ।
संकरस्य च कर्ता स्यामुपहन्यामिमाः प्रजाः ॥ २४
सक्ताः कर्मण्यविद्वांसो यथा कुर्वन्ति भारत ।
कुर्याद्विद्वांस्तथासक्तश्चिकीर्षुर्लोकसंग्रहम् ॥ २५
न बुद्धिभेदं जनयेदज्ञानां कर्मसङ्गिनाम् ।
जोषयेत्सर्वकर्माणि विद्वान्युक्तः समाचरन् ॥ २६
प्रकृतेः क्रियमाणानि गुणैः कर्माणि सर्वशः ।
अहंकारविमूढात्मा कर्ताहमिति मन्यते ॥ २७

But he, O Mighty One, who understands correctly the relation of the Qualities to action, is not attached to the act, for he perceives that it is merely the action and reaction of the Qualities among themselves.

Those who do not understand the Qualities are interested in the act. Still, the wise man who knows the truth should not disturb the mind of him who does not.

Therefore, surrendering thy actions unto Me, thy thoughts concentrated on the Absolute, free from selfishness and without anticipation of reward, with mind devoid of excitement, begin thou to fight.

Those who act always in accordance with My precepts, firm in faith and without cavilling, they too are freed from the bondage of action.

But they who ridicule My word and do not keep it, are ignorant, devoid of wisdom and blind. They seek but their own destruction.

Even the wise man acts in character with his nature; indeed, all creatures act according to their natures. What is the use of compulsion then?

The love and hate which are aroused by the objects of sense arise from Nature; do not yield to them. They only obstruct the path.

It is better to do thine own duty, however lacking in merit, than to do that of another, even though efficiently. It is better to die doing one's own duty, for to do the duty of another is fraught with danger.

तत्त्ववित्तु महाबाहो गुणकर्मविभागयोः ।
गुणा गुणेषु वर्तन्त इति मत्वा न सज्जते ॥ २८
प्रकृतेर्गुणसंमूढाः सज्जन्ते गुणकर्मसु ।
तानकृत्स्नविदो मन्दान्कृत्स्नविन्न विचालयेत् ॥ २९
मयि सर्वाणि कर्माणि संन्यस्याध्यात्मचेतसा ।
निराशीर्निर्ममो भूत्वा युध्यस्व विगतज्वरः ॥ ३०
ये मे मतमिदं नित्यमनुतिष्ठन्ति मानवाः ।
श्रद्धावन्तोऽनसूयन्तो मुच्यन्ते तेऽपि कर्मभिः ॥ ३१
ये त्वेतदभ्यसूयन्तो नानुतिष्ठन्ति मे मतम् ।
सर्वज्ञानविमूढांस्तान्विद्धि नष्टानचेतसः ॥ ३२
सदृशं चेष्टते स्वस्याः प्रकृतेर्ज्ञानवानपि ।
प्रकृतिं यान्ति भूतानि निग्रहः किं करिष्यति ॥ ३३
इन्द्रियस्येन्द्रियस्यार्थे रागद्वेषौ व्यवस्थितौ ।
तयोर्न वशमागच्छेत्तौ ह्यस्य परिपन्थिनौ ॥ ३४
श्रेयान्स्वधर्मो विगुणः परधर्मात्स्वनुष्ठितात् ।
स्वधर्मे निधनं श्रेयः परधर्मो भयावहः ॥ ३५

Arjuna asked: My Lord! Tell me, what is it that drives a man to sin, even against his will and as if by compulsion?

Lord Shri Krishna said: It is desire, it is aversion, born of passion. Desire consumes and corrupts everything. It is man's greatest enemy.

As fire is shrouded in smoke, a mirror by dust and a child by the womb, so is the universe enveloped in desire.

It is the wise man's constant enemy; it tarnishes the face of wisdom. It is as insatiable as a flame of fire.

It works through the senses, the mind and the reason; and with their help destroys wisdom and confounds the soul.

Therefore, O Arjuna, first control thy senses and then slay desire, for it is full of sin, and is the destroyer of knowledge and of wisdom.

It is said that the senses are powerful. But beyond the senses is the mind, beyond mind is intellect, and beyond and greater than intellect is He.

Thus, O Mighty-in-Arms, knowing Him to be beyond the intellect and, by His help, subduing thy personal egotism, kill thine enemy, Desire, extremely difficult though it be."

Thus, in the Holy Book the Bhagavad Gita, one of the Upanishads, in the Science of the Supreme Spirit, in the Art of Self-Knowledge, in the colloquy between the Divine Lord Shri Krishna and the Prince Arjuna, stands the third chapter entitled: Karma-Yoga or the Path of Action.

अर्जुन उवाच ।
अथ केन प्रयुक्तोऽयं पापं चरति पूरुषः ।
अनिच्छन्नपि वार्ष्णेय बलादिव नियोजितः ॥ ३६
श्रीभगवानुवाच ।
काम एष क्रोधः एष रजोगुणसमुद्भवः ।
महाशनो महापाप्मा विद्ध्येनमिह वैरिणम् ॥ ३७
धूमेनाव्रियते वह्निर्यथादर्शो मलेन च ।
यथोल्बेनावृतो गर्भस्तथा तेनेदमावृतम् ॥ ३८
आवृतं ज्ञानमेतेन ज्ञानिनो नित्यवैरिणा ।
कामरूपेण कौन्तेय दुष्पूरेणानलेन च ॥ ३९
इन्द्रियाणि मनो बुद्धिरस्याधिष्ठानमुच्यते ।
एतैर्विमोहयत्येष ज्ञानमावृत्य देहिनम् ॥ ४०
तस्मात्त्वमिन्द्रियाण्यादौ नियम्य भरतर्षभ ।
पाप्मानं प्रजहिह्येनं ज्ञानविज्ञाननाशनम् ॥ ४१
इन्द्रियाणि पराण्याहुरिन्द्रियेभ्यः परं मनः ।
मनसस्तु परा बुद्धिर्यो बुद्धेः परतस्तु सः ॥ ४२
एवं बुद्धेः परं बुद्ध्वा संस्तभ्यात्मानमात्मना ।
जहि शत्रुं महाबाहो कामरूपं दुरासदम् ॥ ४३

इति श्रीमद्भगवद्गीतासु तृतीयोऽध्यायः ॥ ३ ॥

FOUR

·୫·

DNYANA-YOGA
—THE PATH OF WISDOM

श्रीभगवानुवाच ।
इमं विवस्वते योगं प्रोक्तवानहमव्ययम् ।
विवस्वान्मनवे प्राह मनुरिक्ष्वाकवेऽब्रवीत् ॥ १
एवं परंपराप्राप्तमिमं राजर्षयो विदुः ।
स कालेनेह महता योगो नष्टः परंतप ॥ २
स एवायं मया तेऽद्य योगः प्रोक्तः पुरातनः ।
भक्तोऽसि मे सखा चेति रहस्यं ह्येतदुत्तमम् ॥ ३

अर्जुन उवाच ।
अपरं भवतो जन्म परं जन्म विवस्वतः ।
कथमेतद्विजानीयां त्वमादौ प्रोक्तवानिति ॥ ४

श्रीभगवानुवाच ।
बहूनि मे व्यतीतानि जन्मानि तव चार्जुन ।
तान्यहं वेद सर्वाणि न त्वं वेत्थ परंतप ॥ ५
अजोऽपि सन्नव्ययात्मा भूतानामीश्वरोऽपि सन् ।
प्रकृतिं स्वामधिष्ठाय संभवाम्यात्ममायया ॥ ६
यदा यदा हि धर्मस्य ग्लानिर्भवति भारत ।
अभ्युत्थानमधर्मस्य तदात्मानं सृजाम्यहम् ॥ ७
परित्राणाय साधूनां विनाशाय च दुष्कृताम् ।
धर्मसंस्थापनार्थाय संभवामि युगे युगे ॥ ८
जन्म कर्म च मे दिव्यमेवं यो वेत्ति तत्त्वतः ।
त्यक्त्वा देहं पुनर्जन्म नैति मामेति सोऽर्जुन ॥ ९

"*Lord Shri Krishna said:* This imperishable philosophy I taught to Viwaswana, the founder of the Sun dynasty, Viwaswana gave it to Manu the Lawgiver, and Manu to King Ikshwaku!

The Divine Kings knew it, for it was their tradition. Then, after a long time, at last it was forgotten.

It is this same ancient Path that I have now revealed to thee, since thou art My devotee and My friend. It is the supreme Secret.

Arjuna asked: My Lord! Viwaswana was born before Thee; how then canst Thou have revealed it to him?

Lord Shri Krishna replied: I have been born again and again, from time to time; thou too, O Arjuna! My births are known to Me, but thou knowest not thine.

I have no beginning. Though I am imperishable, as well as Lord of all that exists, yet by My own will and power do I manifest Myself.

Whenever spirituality decays and materialism is rampant, then, O Arjuna, I reincarnate Myself!

To protect the righteous, to destroy the wicked and to establish the kingdom of God, I am reborn from age to age.

He who realises the divine truth concerning My birth and life is not born again; and when he leaves his body, he becomes one with Me.

Many have merged their existence in Mine, being freed from desire, fear and anger, filled always with Me and purified by the illuminating flame of self-abnegation.

Howsoever men try to worship Me, so do I welcome them. By whatever path they travel, it leads to Me at last.

Those who look for success, worship the Powers; and in this world their actions bear immediate fruit.

वीतरागभयक्रोधा मन्मया मामुपाश्रिताः ।
बहवो ज्ञानतपसा पूता मद्भावमागताः ॥ १०
ये यथा मां प्रपद्यन्ते तांस्तथैव भजाम्यहम् ।
मम वर्त्मानुवर्तन्ते मनुष्याः पार्थ सर्वशः ॥ ११
काङ्क्षन्तः कर्मणां सिद्धिं यजन्त इह देवताः ।
क्षिप्रं हि मानुषे लोके सिद्धिर्भवति कर्मजा ॥ १२

The four divisions of society (the wise, the soldier, the merchant, the labourer) were created by Me, according to the natural distribution of Qualities and instincts. I am the author of them, though I Myself do no action, and am changeless.

My actions do not fetter Me, nor do I desire anything that they can bring. He who thus realises Me is not enslaved by action.

In the light of this wisdom, our ancestors, who sought deliverance, performed their acts. Act thou also, as did our fathers of old.

What is action and what is inaction? It is a question which has bewildered the wise. But I will declare unto thee the philosophy of action, and knowing it, thou shalt be free from evil.

It is necessary to consider what is right action, what is wrong action, and what is inaction, for mysterious is the law of action.

He who can see inaction in action, and action in inaction, is the wisest among men. He is a saint, even though he still acts.

The wise call him a sage, for whatever he undertakes is free from the motive of desire, and his deeds are purified by the fire of Wisdom.

Having surrendered all claim to the results of his actions, always contented and independent, in reality he does nothing, even though he is apparently acting.

Expecting nothing, his mind and personality controlled, without greed, doing bodily actions only; though he acts, yet he remains untainted.

Content with what comes to him without effort of his own, mounting above the pairs of opposites, free from envy, his mind balanced both in success and failure; though he acts, yet the consequences do not bind him.

He who is without attachment, free, his mind centred in wisdom, his actions, being done as a sacrifice, leave no trace behind.

For him, the sacrifice itself is the Spirit; the Spirit and the oblation are one; it is the Spirit Itself which is sacrificed in Its own fire, and the man even in action is united with God, since while performing his act, his mind never ceases to be fixed on Him.

चातुर्वर्ण्यं मया सृष्टं गुणकर्मविभागशः ।
तस्य कर्तारमपि मां विद्ध्यकर्तारमव्ययम् ॥ १३

न मां कर्माणि लिम्पन्ति न मे कर्मफले स्पृहा ।
इति मां योऽभिजानाति कर्मभिर्न स बध्यते ॥ १४

एवं ज्ञात्वा कृतं कर्म पूर्वैरपि मुमुक्षुभिः ।
कुरु कर्मैव तस्मात्त्वं पूर्वैः पूर्वतरं कृतम् ॥ १५

किं कर्म किमकर्मेति कवयोऽप्यत्र मोहिताः ।
तत्ते कर्म प्रवक्ष्यामि यज्ज्ञात्वा मोक्ष्यसेऽशुभात् ॥ १६

कर्मणो ह्यपि बोद्धव्यं बोद्धव्यं च विकर्मणः ।
अकर्मणश्च बोद्धव्यं गहना कर्मणो गतिः ॥ १७

कर्मण्यकर्म यः पश्येदकर्मणि च कर्म यः ।
स बुद्धिमान्मनुष्येषु स युक्तः कृत्स्नकर्मकृत् ॥ १८

यस्य सर्वे समारम्भाः कामसंकल्पवर्जिताः ।
ज्ञानाग्निदग्धकर्माणं तमाहुः पण्डितं बुधाः ॥ १९

त्यक्त्वा कर्मफलासङ्गं नित्यतृप्तो निराश्रयः ।
कर्मण्यभिप्रवृत्तोऽपि नैव किंचित्करोति सः ॥ २०

निराशीर्यतचित्तात्मा त्यक्तसर्वपरिग्रहः ।
शारीरं केवलं कर्म कुर्वन्नाप्नोति किल्बिषम् ॥ २१

यदृच्छालाभसंतुष्टो द्वंद्वातीतो विमत्सरः ।
समः सिद्धावसिद्धौ च कृत्वापि न निबध्यते ॥ २२

गतसङ्गस्य मुक्तस्य ज्ञानावस्थितचेतसः ।
यज्ञायाचरतः कर्म समग्रं प्रविलीयते ॥ २३

ब्रह्मार्पणं ब्रह्म हविर्ब्रह्माग्नौ ब्रह्मणा हुतम् ।
ब्रह्मैव तेन गन्तव्यं ब्रह्मकर्मसमाधिना ॥ २४

दैवमेवापरे यज्ञं योगिनः पर्युपासते ।
ब्रह्माग्नावपरे यज्ञं यज्ञेनैवोपजुह्वति ॥ २५
श्रोत्रादीनीन्द्रियाण्यन्ये संयमाग्निषु जुह्वति ।
शब्दादीन्विषयानन्य इन्द्रियाग्निषु जुह्वति ॥ २६
सर्वाणीन्द्रियकर्माणि प्राणकर्माणि चापरे ।
आत्मसंयमयोगाग्नौ जुह्वति ज्ञानदीपिते ॥ २७
द्रव्ययज्ञास्तपोयज्ञा योगयज्ञास्तथापरे ।
स्वाध्यायज्ञानयज्ञाश्च यतयः संशितव्रताः ॥ २८
अपाने जुह्वति प्राणं प्राणेऽपानं तथापरे ।
प्राणापानगती रुद्ध्वा प्राणायामपरायणाः ॥ २९
अपरे नियताहाराः प्राणान्प्राणेषु जुह्वति ।
सर्वेऽप्येते यज्ञविदो यज्ञक्षपितकल्मषाः ॥ ३०
यज्ञशिष्टामृतभुजो यान्ति ब्रह्म सनातनम् ।
नायं लोकोऽस्त्ययज्ञस्य कुतोऽन्यः कुरुसत्तम ॥ ३१

Some sages sacrifice to the Powers; others offer themselves on the altar of the Eternal.

Some sacrifice their physical senses in the fire of self-control; others offer up their contact with external objects in the sacrificial fire of their senses.

Others again sacrifice their activities and their vitality in the Spiritual fire of self-abnegation, kindled by wisdom.

And yet others offer as their sacrifice wealth, austerities and meditation. Monks wedded to their vows renounce their scriptural learning and even their spiritual powers.

There are some who practise control of the Vital Energy and govern the subtle forces of Prana and Apana, thereby sacrificing their Prana unto Apana, or their Apana unto Prana.

Others, controlling their diet, sacrifice their worldly life to the spiritual fire. All understand the principle of sacrifice, and by its means their sins are washed away.

Tasting the nectar of immortality, as the reward of sacrifice, they reach the Eternal. This world is not for those who refuse to sacrifice; much less the other world.

एवं बहुविधा यज्ञा वितता ब्रह्मणो मुखे ।
कर्मजान्विद्धि तान्सर्वानेवं ज्ञात्वा विमोक्ष्यसे ॥ ३२

श्रेयान्द्रव्यमयाद्यज्ञाज्ज्ञानयज्ञः परंतप ।
सर्वं कर्माखिलं पार्थ ज्ञाने परिसमाप्यते ॥ ३३

तद्विद्धि प्रणिपातेन परिप्रश्नेन सेवया ।
उपदेक्ष्यन्ति ते ज्ञानं ज्ञानिनस्तत्त्वदर्शिनः ॥ ३४

यज्ज्ञात्वा न पुनर्मोहमेवं यास्यसि पाण्डव ।
येन भूतान्यशेषेण द्रक्ष्यस्यात्मन्यथो मयि ॥ ३५

अपि चेदसि पापेभ्यः सर्वेभ्यः पापकृत्तमः ।
सर्वं ज्ञानप्लवेनैव वृजिनं संतरिष्यसि ॥ ३६

यथैधांसि समिद्धोऽग्निर्भस्मसात्कुरुतेऽर्जुन ।
ज्ञानाग्निः सर्वकर्माणि भस्मसात्कुरुते तथा ॥ ३७

न हि ज्ञानेन सदृशं पवित्रमिह विद्यते ।
तत्स्वयं योगसंसिद्धः कालेनात्मनि विन्दति ॥ ३८

In this way other sacrifices too may be undergone for the Spirit's sake. Know thou that they all depend on action. Knowing this, thou shalt be free.

The sacrifice of wisdom is superior to any material sacrifice, for, O Arjuna, the climax of action is always Realisation.

This shalt thou learn by prostrating thyself at the Master's feet, by questioning Him and by serving Him. The wise who have realised the Truth will teach thee wisdom.

Having known That, thou shalt never again be confounded; and, O Arjuna, by the power of that wisdom, thou shalt see all these people as if they were thine own Self, and therefore as Me.

Be thou the greatest of all sinners, yet thou shalt cross over all sin by the ferryboat of wisdom.

As the kindled fire consumes the fuel, so, O Arjuna, in the flame of wisdom the embers of action are burnt to ashes.

There is nothing in the world so purifying as wisdom; and he who is a perfect saint finds that at last in his own Self.

He who is full of faith attains wisdom, and he too who can control his senses. Having attained that wisdom, he shall ere long attain the Supreme Peace.

But the ignorant man, and he who has no faith, and the sceptic are lost. Neither in this world nor elsewhere is there any happiness in store for him who always doubts.

But the man who has renounced his action for meditation, who has cleft his doubt in twain by the sword of wisdom, who remains always enthroned in his Self, is not bound by his acts.

Therefore, cleaving asunder with the sword of wisdom the doubts of thy heart, which thine own ignorance has engendered, follow the Path of Wisdom and arise!"

Thus, in the Holy Book the Bhagavad Gita, one of the Upanishads, in the Science of the Supreme Spirit, in the Art of Self-Knowledge, in the colloquy between the Divine Lord Shri Krishna and the Prince Arjuna, stands the fourth chapter, entitled: Dnyana-Yoga or the Path of Wisdom.

श्रद्धावाँल्लभते ज्ञानं तत्परः संयतेन्द्रियः ।
ज्ञानं लब्ध्वा परां शान्तिमचिरेणाधिगच्छति ॥ ३९
अज्ञश्चाश्रद्दधानश्च संशयात्मा विनश्यति ।
नायं लोकोऽस्ति न परो न सुखं संशयात्मनः ॥ ४०
योगसंन्यस्तकर्माणं ज्ञानसंछिन्नसंशयम् ।
आत्मवन्तं न कर्माणि निबध्नन्ति धनंजय ॥ ४१
तस्मादज्ञानसंभूतं हृत्स्थं ज्ञानासिनात्मनः ।
छित्त्वैनं संशयं योगमातिष्ठोत्तिष्ठ भारत ॥ ४२

इति श्रीमद्भगवद्गीतासु चतुर्थोऽध्यायः ॥ ४ ॥

FIVE

•५•

THE RENUNCIATION OF ACTION

अर्जुन उवाच ।
संन्यासं कर्मणां कृष्ण पुनर्योगं च शंससि ।
यच्छ्रेय एतयोरेकं तन्मे ब्रूहि सुनिश्चितम् ॥ १
श्रीभगवानुवाच ।
संन्यासः कर्मयोगश्च निःश्रेयसकरावुभौ ।
तयोस्तु कर्मसंन्यासात्कर्मयोगो विशिष्यते ॥ २
ज्ञेयः स नित्यसंन्यासी यो न द्वेष्टि न काङ्क्षति ।
निर्द्वन्द्वो हि महाबाहो सुखं बन्धात्प्रमुच्यते ॥ ३
सांख्ययोगौ पृथग्बालाः प्रवदन्ति न पण्डिताः ।
एकमप्यास्थितः सम्यगुभयोर्विन्दते फलम् ॥ ४
यत्सांख्यैः प्राप्यते स्थानं तद्योगैरपि गम्यते ।
एकं सांख्यं च योगं च यः पश्यति स पश्यति ॥ ५
संन्यासस्तु महाबाहो दुःखमाप्तुमयोगतः ।
योगयुक्तो मुनिर्ब्रह्म नचिरेणाधिगच्छति ॥ ६
योगयुक्तो विशुद्धात्मा विजितात्मा जितेन्द्रियः ।
सर्वभूतात्मभूतात्मा कुर्वन्नपि न लिप्यते ॥ ७

"*Arjuna said:* My Lord! At one moment Thou praisest renunciation of action; at another, right action. Tell me truly, I pray, which of these is the more conducive to my highest welfare?

Lord Shri Krishna replied: Renunciation of action and the path of right action both lead to the highest; of the two, right action is the better.

He is a true ascetic who never desires or dislikes, who is uninfluenced by the opposites and is easily freed from bondage.

Only the unenlightened speak of wisdom and right action as separate, not the wise. If any man knows one, he enjoys the fruit of both.

The level which is reached by wisdom is attained through right action as well. He who perceives that the two are one, knows the truth.

Without concentration, O Mighty Man, renunciation is difficult. But the sage who is always meditating on the Divine, before long shall attain the Absolute.

He who is spiritual, who is pure, who has overcome his senses and his personal self, who has realised his highest Self as the Self of all, such a one, even though he acts, is not bound by his acts.

Though the saint sees, hears, touches, smells, eats, moves, sleeps and breathes, yet he knows the Truth, and he knows that it is not he who acts.

Though he talks, though he gives and receives, though he opens his eyes and shuts them, he still knows that his senses are merely disporting themselves among the objects of perception.

He who dedicates his actions to the Spirit, without any personal attachment to them, he is no more tainted by sin than the water lily is wetted by water.

The sage performs his action dispassionately, using his body, mind and intellect, and even his senses, always as a means of purification.

Having abandoned the fruit of action, he wins eternal peace. Others unacquainted with spirituality, led by desire and clinging to the benefit which they think will follow their actions, become entangled by them.

Mentally renouncing all actions, the self-controlled soul enjoys bliss in this body, the city of the nine gates, neither doing anything himself nor causing anything to be done.

The Lord of this universe has not ordained activity, or any incentive thereto, or any relation between an act and its consequences. All this is the work of Nature.

नैव किंचित्करोमीति युक्तो मन्येत तत्त्ववित् ।
पश्यञ्शृण्वन्स्पृशञ्जिघ्रन्नश्नन्गच्छन्स्वपञ्श्वसन् ॥ ८
प्रलपन्विसृजन्गृह्णन्नुन्मिषन्निमिषन्नपि ।
इन्द्रियाणीन्द्रियार्थेषु वर्तन्त इति धारयन् ॥ ९
ब्रह्मण्याधाय कर्माणि सङ्गं त्यक्त्वा करोति यः ।
लिप्यते न स पापेन पद्मपत्रमिवाम्भसा ॥ १०
कायेन मनसा बुद्ध्या केवलैरिन्द्रियैरपि ।
योगिनः कर्म कुर्वन्ति सङ्गं त्यक्त्वात्मशुद्धये ॥ ११
युक्तः कर्मफलं त्यक्त्वा शान्तिमाप्नोति नैष्ठिकीम् ।
अयुक्तः कामकारेण फले सक्तो निबध्यते ॥ १२
सर्वकर्माणि मनसा संन्यस्यास्ते सुखं वशी ।
नवद्वारे पुरे देही नैव कुर्वन्न कारयन् ॥ १३
न कर्तृत्वं न कर्माणि लोकस्य सृजति प्रभुः ।
न कर्मफलसंयोगं स्वभावस्तु प्रवर्तते ॥ १४

The Lord does not accept responsibility for any man's sin or merit. Men are deluded because in them wisdom is submerged in ignorance.

Surely wisdom is like the sun, revealing the supreme truth to those whose ignorance is dispelled by the wisdom of the Self.

Meditating on the Divine, having faith in the Divine, concentrating on the Divine and losing themselves in the Divine, their sins dissolved in wisdom, they go whence there is no return.

Sages look equally upon all, whether he be a minister of learning and humility, or an infidel, or whether it be a cow, an elephant or a dog.

Even in this world they conquer their earth-life whose minds, fixed on the Supreme, remain always balanced; for the Supreme has neither blemish nor bias.

He who knows and lives in the Absolute remains unmoved and unperturbed; he is not elated by pleasure or depressed by pain.

He finds happiness in his own Self, and enjoys eternal bliss, whose heart does not yearn for the contacts of earth and whose Self is one with the Everlasting.

नादत्ते कस्यचित्पापं न चैव सुकृतं विभुः ।
अज्ञानेनावृतं ज्ञानं तेन मुह्यन्ति जन्तवः ॥ १५
ज्ञानेन तु तदज्ञानं येषां नाशितमात्मनः ।
तेषामादित्यवज्ज्ञानं प्रकाशयति तत्परम् ॥ १६
तद्बुद्धयस्तदात्मानस्तन्निष्ठास्तत्परायणाः ।
गच्छन्त्यपुनरावृत्तिं ज्ञाननिर्धूतकल्मषाः ॥ १७
विद्याविनयसंपन्ने ब्राह्मणे गवि हस्तिनि ।
शुनि चैव श्वपाके च पण्डिताः समदर्शिनः ॥ १८
इहैव तैर्जितः सर्गो येषां साम्ये स्थितं मनः ।
निर्दोषं हि समं ब्रह्म तस्माद्ब्रह्मणि ते स्थिताः ॥ १९
न प्रहृष्येत्प्रियं प्राप्य नोद्विजेत्प्राप्य चाप्रियम् ।
स्थिरबुद्धिरसंमूढो ब्रह्मविद्ब्रह्मणि स्थितः ॥ २०
बाह्यस्पर्शेष्वसक्तात्मा विन्दत्यात्मनि यत्सुखम् ।
स ब्रह्मयोगयुक्तात्मा सुखमक्षयमश्नुते ॥ २१

The joys that spring from external associations bring pain; they have their beginnings and their endings. The wise man does not rejoice in them.

He who, before he leaves his body, learns to surmount the promptings of desire and anger is a saint and is happy.

He who is happy within his Self and has found Its peace, and in whom the inner light shines, that sage attains Eternal Bliss and becomes the Spirit Itself.

Sages whose sins have been washed away, whose sense of separateness has vanished, who have subdued themselves, and seek only the welfare of all, come to the Eternal Spirit.

Saints who know their Selves, who control their minds, and feel neither desire nor anger, find Eternal Bliss everywhere.

Excluding external objects, his gaze fixed between the eyebrows, the inward and outward breathings passing equally through his nostrils;

Governing sense, mind and intellect, intent on liberation, free from desire, fear and anger, the sage is forever free.

Knowing me as Him who gladly receives all offerings of austerity and sacrifice, as the Mighty Ruler of all the Worlds and the Friend of all beings, he passes to Eternal Peace."

Thus, in the Holy Book the Bhagavad Gita, one of the Upanishads, in the Science of the Supreme Spirit, in the Art of Self-Knowledge, in the colloquy between the Divine Lord Shri Krishna and the Prince Arjuna, stands the fifth chapter, entitled: The Renunciation of Action.

ये हि संस्पर्शजा भोगा दुःखयोनय एव ते ।
आद्यन्तवन्तः कौन्तेय न तेषु रमते बुधः ॥ २२

शक्नोतीहैव यः सोढुं प्राक्शरीरविमोक्षणात् ।
कामक्रोधोद्भवं वेगं स युक्तः स सुखी नरः ॥ २३

योऽन्तःसुखोऽन्तरारामस्तथान्तज्र्योतिरेव यः ।
स योगी ब्रह्मनिर्वाणं ब्रह्मभूतोऽधिगच्छति ॥ २४

लभन्ते ब्रह्मनिर्वाणमृषयः क्षीणकल्मषाः ।
छिन्नद्वैधा यतात्मानः सर्वभूतहिते रताः ॥ २५

कामक्रोधवियुक्तानां यतीनां यतचेतसाम् ।
अभितो ब्रह्मनिर्वाणं वर्तते विदितात्मनाम् ॥ २६

स्पर्शान्कृत्वा बहिर्बाह्यांश्चक्षुश्चैवान्तरे भ्रुवोः ।
प्राणापानौ समौ कृत्वा नासाभ्यन्तरचारिणौ ॥ २७

यतेन्द्रियमनोबुद्धिर्मुनिर्मोक्षपरायणः ।
विगतेच्छाभयक्रोधो यः सदा मुक्त एव सः ॥ २८

भोक्तारं यज्ञतपसां सर्वलोकमहेश्वरम् ।
सुहृदं सर्वभूतानां ज्ञात्वा मां शान्तिमृच्छति ॥ २९

इति श्रीमद्भगवद्गीतासु पञ्चमोऽध्यायः ॥ ५ ॥

SIX
·&·
SELF-CONTROL

"*Lord Shri Krishna said:* He who acts because it is his duty, not thinking of the consequences, is really spiritual and a true ascetic; and not he who merely observes rituals or who shuns all action.

O Arjuna! Renunciation is in fact what is called Right Action. No one can become spiritual who has not renounced all desire.

For the sage who seeks the heights of spiritual meditation, practice is the only method, and when he has attained them, he must maintain himself there by continual self-control.

When a man renounces even the thought of initiating action, when he is not interested in sense objects or any results which may flow from his acts, then in truth he understands spirituality.

Let him seek liberation by the help of his highest Self, and let him never disgrace his own Self. For that Self is his only friend; yet it may also be his enemy.

To him who has conquered his lower nature by Its help, the Self is a friend, but to him who has not done so, It is an enemy.

The Self of him who is self-controlled and has attained peace is equally unmoved by heat or cold, pleasure or pain, honour or dishonour.

He who desires nothing but wisdom and spiritual insight, who has conquered his senses and who looks with the same eye upon a lump of earth, a stone or fine gold, is the real saint.

He looks impartially on all—lover, friend or foe; indifferent or hostile; alien or relative; virtuous or sinful.

श्रीभगवानुवाच ।
अनाश्रितः कर्मफलं कार्यं कर्म करोति यः ।
स संन्यासी च योगी च न निरग्निर्न चाक्रियः ॥ १
यं संन्यासमिति प्राहुर्योगं तं विद्धि पाण्डव ।
न ह्यसंन्यस्तसंकल्पो योगी भवति कश्चन ॥ २
आरुरुक्षोर्मुनेर्योगं कर्म कारणमुच्यते ।
योगारूढस्य तस्यैव शमः कारणमुच्यते ॥ ३
यदा हि नेन्द्रियार्थेषु न कर्मस्वनुषज्जते ।
सर्वसंकल्पसंन्यासी योगारूढस्तदोच्यते ॥ ४
उद्धरेदात्मनात्मानं नात्मानमवसादयेत् ।
आत्मैव ह्यात्मनो बन्धुरात्मैव रिपुरात्मनः ॥ ५
बन्धुरात्मात्मनस्तस्य येनात्मैवात्मना जितः ।
अनात्मनस्तु शत्रुत्वे वर्तेतात्मैव शत्रुवत् ॥ ६
जितात्मनः प्रशान्तस्य परमात्मा समाहितः ।
शीतोष्णसुखदुःखेषु तथा मानावमानयोः ॥ ७
ज्ञानविज्ञानतृप्तात्मा कूटस्थो विजितेन्द्रियः ।
युक्त इत्युच्यते योगी समलोष्टाश्मकाञ्चनः ॥ ८
सुहृन्मित्रार्युदासीनमध्यस्थद्वेष्यबन्धुषु ।
साधुष्वपि च पापेषु समबुद्धिर्विशिष्यते ॥ ९

योगी युञ्जीत सततमात्मानं रहसि स्थितः ।
एकाकी यतचित्तात्मा निराशीरपरिग्रहः ॥ १०
शुचौ देशे प्रतिष्ठाप्य स्थिरमासनमात्मनः ।
नात्युच्छ्रितं नातिनीचं चैलाजिनकुशोत्तरम् ॥ ११
तत्रैकाग्रं मनः कृत्वा यतचित्तेन्द्रियक्रियः ।
उपविश्यासने युञ्ज्याद्योगमात्मविशुद्धये ॥ १२
समं कायशिरोग्रीवं धारयन्नचलं स्थिरः ।
संप्रेक्ष्य नासिकाग्रं स्वं दिशश्चानवलोकयन् ॥ १३
प्रशान्तात्मा विगतभीर्ब्रह्मचारिव्रते स्थितः ।
मनः संयम्य मच्चित्तो युक्त आसीत मत्परः ॥ १४
युञ्जन्नेवं सदात्मानं योगी नियतमानसः ।
शान्तिं निर्वाणपरमां मत्संस्थामधिगच्छति ॥ १५

Let the student of spirituality try unceasingly to concentrate his mind; let him live in seclusion, absolutely alone, with mind and personality controlled, free from desire and without possessions.

Having chosen a holy place, let him sit in a firm posture on a seat, neither too high nor too low, and covered with a grass mat, a deer skin and a cloth.

Seated thus, his mind concentrated, its functions controlled and his senses governed, let him practise meditation for the purification of his lower nature.

Let him hold body, head and neck erect, motionless and steady; let him look fixedly at the tip of his nose, turning neither to the right nor to the left.

With peace in his heart and no fear, observing the vow of celibacy, with mind controlled and fixed on Me, let the student lose himself in contemplation of Me.

Thus keeping his mind always in communion with Me, and with his thoughts subdued, he shall attain that Peace which is Mine and which will lead him to liberation at last.

नात्यश्नतस्तु योगोऽस्ति न चैकान्तमनश्नतः ।
न चातिस्वप्नशीलस्य जाग्रतो नैव चार्जुन ॥ १६
युक्ताहारविहारस्य युक्तचेष्टस्य कर्मसु ।
युक्तस्वप्नावबोधस्य योगो भवति दुःखहा ॥ १७
यदा विनियतं चित्तमात्मन्येवावतिष्ठते ।
निःस्पृहः सर्वकामेभ्यो युक्त इत्युच्यते तदा ॥ १८
यथा दीपो निवातस्थो नेङ्गते सोपमा स्मृता ।
योगिनो यतचित्तस्य युञ्जतो योगमात्मनः ॥ १९
यत्रोपरमते चित्तं निरुद्धं योगसेवया ।
यत्र चैवात्मनात्मानं पश्यन्नात्मनि तुष्यति ॥ २०

Meditation is not for him who eats too much, nor for him who eats not at all; nor for him who is overmuch addicted to sleep, nor for him who is always awake.

But for him who regulates his food and recreation, who is balanced in action, in sleep and in waking, it shall dispel all unhappiness.

When the mind, completely controlled, is centred in the Self, and free from all earthly desires, then is the man truly spiritual.

The wise man who has conquered his mind and is absorbed in the Self is as a lamp which does not flicker, since it stands sheltered from every wind.

There, where the whole nature is seen in the light of the Self, where the man abides within his Self and is satisfied, there, its functions restrained by its union with the Divine, the mind finds rest.

सुखमात्यन्तिकं यत्तद्बुद्धिग्राह्यमतीन्द्रियम् ।
वेत्ति यत्र न चैवायं स्थितश्चलति तत्त्वतः ॥ २१
यं लब्ध्वा चापरं लाभं मन्यते नाधिकं ततः ।
यस्मिन्स्थितो न दुःखेन गुरुणापि विचाल्यते ॥ २२
तं विद्याद्दुःखसंयोगवियोगं योगसंज्ञितम् ।
स निश्चयेन योक्तव्यो योगोऽनिर्विण्णचेतसा ॥ २३
संकल्पप्रभवान्कामांस्त्यक्त्वा सर्वानशेषतः ।
मनसैवेन्द्रियग्रामं विनियम्य समन्ततः ॥ २४
शनैः शनैरुपरमेद्बुद्ध्या धृतिगृहीतया ।
आत्मसंस्थं मनः कृत्वा न किंचिदपि चिन्तयेत् ॥ २५
यतो यतो निश्चरति मनश्चञ्चलमस्थिरम् ।
ततस्ततो नियम्यैतदात्मन्येव वशं नयेत् ॥ २६
प्रशान्तमनसं ह्येनं योगिनं सुखमुत्तमम् ।
उपैति शान्तरजसं ब्रह्मभूतमकल्मषम् ॥ २७
युञ्जन्नेवं सदात्मानं योगी विगतकल्मषः ।
सुखेन ब्रह्मसंस्पर्शमत्यन्तं सुखमश्नुते ॥ २८
सर्वभूतस्थमात्मानं सर्वभूतानि चात्मनि ।
ईक्षते योगयुक्तात्मा सर्वत्र समदर्शनः ॥ २९
यो मां पश्यति सर्वत्र सर्वं च मयि पश्यति ।
तस्याहं न प्रणश्यामि स च मे न प्रणश्यति ॥ ३०
सर्वभूतस्थितं यो मां भजत्येकत्वमास्थितः ।
सर्वथा वर्तमानोऽपि स योगी मयि वर्तते ॥ ३१
आत्मौपम्येन सर्वत्र समं पश्यति योऽर्जुन ।
सुखं वा यदि वा दुःखं स योगी परमो मतः ॥ ३२

When he enjoys the Bliss which passes sense, and which only the Pure Intellect can grasp, when he comes to rest within his own highest Self, never again will he stray from reality.

Finding That, he will realise that there is no possession so precious. And when once established there, no calamity can disturb him.

This inner severance from the affliction of misery is spirituality. It should be practised with determination and with a heart which refuses to be depressed.

Renouncing every desire which imagination can conceive, controlling the senses at every point by the power of mind;

Little by little, by the help of his reason controlled by fortitude, let him attain peace; and, fixing his mind on the Self, let him not think of any other thing.

When the volatile and wavering mind would wander, let him restrain it and bring it again to its allegiance to the Self.

Supreme Bliss is the lot of the sage, whose mind attains Peace, whose passions subside, who is without sin, and who becomes one with the Absolute.

Thus, free from sin, abiding always in the Eternal, the saint enjoys without effort the Bliss which flows from realisation of the Infinite.

He who experiences the unity of life sees his own Self in all beings, and all beings in his own Self, and looks on everything with an impartial eye;

He who sees Me in everything and everything in Me, him shall I never forsake, nor shall he lose Me.

The sage who realises the unity of life and who worships Me in all beings, lives in Me, whatever may be his lot.

O Arjuna! He is the perfect saint who, taught by the likeness within himself, sees the same Self everywhere, whether the outer form be pleasurable or painful.

अर्जुन उवाच ।
योऽयं योगस्त्वया प्रोक्तः साम्येन मधुसूदन ।
एतस्याहं न पश्यामि चञ्चलत्वास्थितिं स्थिराम् ॥ ३३
चञ्चलं हि मनः कृष्ण प्रमाथि बलवद्दृढम् ।
तस्याहं निग्रहं मन्ये वायोरिव सुदुष्करम् ॥ ३४
      श्रीभगवानुवाच ।
असंशयं महाबाहो मनो दुर्निग्रहं चलम् ।
अभ्यासेन तु कौन्तेय वैराग्येण च गृह्यते ॥ ३५
असंयतात्मना योगो दुष्प्राप इति मे मतिः ।
वश्यात्मना तु यतता शक्योऽवाप्तुमुपायतः ॥ ३६
      अर्जुन उवाच ।
अयतिः श्रद्धयोपेतो योगाच्चलितमानसः ।
अप्राप्य योगसंसिद्धिं कां गतिं कृष्ण गच्छति ॥ ३७
कच्चिन्नोभयविभ्रष्टश्छिन्नाभ्रमिव नश्यति ।
अप्रतिष्ठो महाबाहो विमूढो ब्रह्मणः पथि ॥ ३८
एतन्मे संशयं कृष्ण छेत्तुमर्हस्यशेषतः ।
त्वदन्यः संशयस्यास्य छेत्ता न ह्युपपद्यते ॥ ३९

Arjuna said: I do not see how I can attain this state of equanimity which Thou hast revealed, owing to the restlessness of my mind.

My Lord! Verily, the mind is fickle and turbulent, obstinate and strong, yea extremely difficult as the wind to control.

Lord Shri Krishna replied: Doubtless, O Mighty One, the mind is fickle and exceedingly difficult to restrain, but, O son of Kunti, with practice and renunciation it can be done.

It is not possible to attain Self-Realisation if a man does not know how to control himself; but for him who, striving by proper means, learns such control, it is possible.

Arjuna asked: He who fails to control himself, whose mind falls from spiritual contemplation, who attains not perfection but retains his faith, what of him, my Lord?

Having failed in both, my Lord, is he without hope, like a riven cloud having no support, lost on the spiritual road?

My Lord! Thou art worthy to solve this doubt once and for all; save Thyself there is no one competent to do so.

Lord Shri Krishna replied: My beloved child! There is no destruction for him, either in this world or in the next. No evil fate awaits him who treads the path of righteousness.

Having reached the worlds where the righteous dwell, and having remained there for many years, he who has slipped away from the path of spirituality will be born again in the family of the pure, benevolent and prosperous.

Or, he may be born in the family of the wise sages, though a birth like this is, indeed, very difficult to obtain.

Then the experience acquired in his former life will revive, and with its help he will strive for perfection more eagerly than before.

Unconsciously he will return to the practices of his old life; so that he who tries to realise spiritual consciousness is certainly superior to one who only talks of it.

Then, after many lives, the student of spirituality, who earnestly strives, and whose sins are absolved, attains perfection and reaches the Supreme.

The wise man is superior to the ascetic and to the scholar and to the man of action; therefore be thou a wise man, O Arjuna!

I look upon him as the best of mystics who, full of faith, worshippeth Me and abideth in Me."

Thus, in the Holy Book the Bhagavad Gita, one of the Upanishads, in the Science of the Supreme Spirit, in the Art of Self-Knowledge, in the colloquy between the Divine Lord Shri Krishna and the Prince Arjuna, stands the sixth chapter, entitled: Self-Control.

श्रीभगवानुवाच ।
पार्थ नैवेह नामुत्र विनाशस्तस्य विद्यते ।
न हि कल्याणकृत्कश्चिद्दुर्गतिं तात गच्छति ॥ ४०
प्राप्य पुण्यकृताँल्लोकानुषित्वा शाश्वतीः समाः ।
शुचीनां श्रीमतां गेहे योगभ्रष्टोऽभिजायते ॥ ४१
अथ वा योगिनामेव कुले भवति धीमताम् ।
एतद्धि दुर्लभतरं लोके जन्म यदीदृशम् ॥ ४२
तत्र तं बुद्धिसंयोगं लभते पौर्वदेहिकम् ।
यतते च ततो भूयः संसिद्धौ कुरुनन्दन ॥ ४३
पूर्वाभ्यासेन तेनैव ह्रियते ह्यवशोऽपि सः ।
जिज्ञासुरपि योगस्य शब्दब्रह्मातिवर्तते ॥ ४४
प्रयत्नाद्यतमानस्तु योगी संशुद्धकिल्बिषः ।
अनेकजन्मसंसिद्धस्ततो याति परां गतिम् ॥ ४५
तपस्विभ्योऽधिको योगी ज्ञानिभ्योऽपि मतोऽधिकः ।
कर्मिभ्यश्चाधिको योगी तस्माद्योगी भवार्जुन ॥ ४६
योगिनामपि सर्वेषां मद्गतेनान्तरात्मना ।
श्रद्धावान्भजते यो मां स मे युक्ततमो मतः ॥ ४७

इति श्रीमद्भगवद्गीतासु षष्ठोऽध्यायः ॥ ६ ॥

SEVEN

٠٧٠

KNOWLEDGE AND EXPERIENCE

श्रीभगवानुवाच ।
मय्यासक्तमनाः पार्थ योगं युञ्जन्मदाश्रयः ।
असंशयं समग्रं मां यथा ज्ञास्यसि तच्छृणु ॥ १
ज्ञानं तेऽहं सविज्ञानमिदं वक्ष्याम्यशेषतः ।
यज्ज्ञात्वा नेह भूयोऽन्यज्ज्ञातव्यमवशिष्यते ॥ २
मनुष्याणां सहस्रेषु कश्चिद्यतति सिद्धये ।
यततामपि सिद्धानां कश्चिन्मां वेत्ति तत्त्वतः ॥ ३
भूमिरापोऽनलो वायुः खं मनो बुद्धिरेव च ।
अहंकार इतीयं मे भिन्ना प्रकृतिरष्टधा ॥ ४
अपरेयमितस्त्वन्यां प्रकृतिं विद्धि मे पराम् ।
जीवभूतां महाबाहो ययेदं धार्यते जगत् ॥ ५
एतद्योनीनि भूतानि सर्वाणीत्युपधारय ।
अहं कृत्स्नस्य जगतः प्रभवः प्रलयस्तथा ॥ ६
मत्तः परतरं नान्यत्किञ्चिदस्ति धनंजय ।
मयि सर्वमिदं प्रोतं सूत्रे मणिगणा इव ॥ ७
रसोऽहमप्सु कौन्तेय प्रभास्मि शशिसूर्ययोः ।
प्रणवः सर्ववेदेषु शब्दः खे पौरुषं नृषु ॥ ८
पुण्यो गन्धः पृथिव्यां च तेजश्चास्मि विभावसौ ।
जीवनं सर्वभूतेषु तपश्चास्मि तपस्विषु ॥ ९
बीजं मां सर्वभूतानां विद्धि पार्थ सनातनम् ।
बुद्धिर्बुद्धिमतामस्मि तेजस्तेजस्विनामहम् ॥ १०
बलं बलवतां चाहं कामरागविवर्जितम् ।
धर्माविरुद्धो भूतेषु कामोऽस्मि भरतर्षभ ॥ ११
ये चैव सात्त्विका भावा राजसास्तामसाश्च ये ।
मत्त एवेति तान्विद्धि न त्वहं तेषु ते मयि ॥ १२
त्रिभिर्गुणमयैर्भावैरेभिः सर्वमिदं जगत् ।
मोहितं नाभिजानाति मामेभ्यः परमव्ययम् ॥ १३

"*Lord Shri Krishna said:* Listen, O Arjuna! And I will tell thee how thou shalt know Me in My full perfection, practising meditation with thy mind devoted to Me, and having Me for thy refuge.

I will reveal this knowledge unto thee, and how it may be realised; which, once accomplished, there remains nothing else worth having in this life.

Among thousands of men scarcely one strives for perfection, and even amongst those who gain occult powers, perchance but one knows Me in truth.

Earth, water, fire, air, ether, mind, intellect and personality; this is the eightfold division of My Manifested Nature.

This is My inferior Nature; but distinct from this, O Valiant One, know thou that my Superior Nature is the very Life which sustains the universe.

It is the womb of all being; for I am He by Whom the worlds were created and shall be dissolved.

O Arjuna! There is nothing higher than Me; all is strung upon Me as rows of pearls upon a thread.

O Arjuna! I am the Fluidity in water, the Light in the sun and in the moon. I am the mystic syllable Om in the Vedic scriptures, the Sound in ether, the Virility in man.

I am the Fragrance of earth, the Brilliance of fire. I am the Life Force in all beings, and I am the Austerity of the ascetics.

Know, O Arjuna, that I am the eternal Seed of being; I am the Intelligence of the intelligent, the Splendour of the resplendent.

I am the Strength of the strong, of them who are free from attachment and desire; and, O Arjuna, I am the Desire for righteousness.

Whatever be the nature of their life, whether it be pure or passionate or ignorant, they all are derived from Me. They are in Me, but I am not in them.

The inhabitants of this world, misled by those natures which the Qualities have engendered, know not that I am higher than them all, and that I do not change.

देवी ह्येषा गुणमयी मम माया दुरत्यया ।
मामेव ये प्रपद्यन्ते मायामेतां तरन्ति ते ॥ १४

न मां दुष्कृतिनो मूढाः प्रपद्यन्ते नराधमाः ।
मायया पहृतज्ञाना आसुरं भावमाश्रिताः ॥ १५

चतुर्विधा भजन्ते मां जनाः सुकृतिनोऽर्जुन ।
आर्तो जिज्ञासुरर्थार्थी ज्ञानी च भरतर्षभ ॥ १६

तेषां ज्ञानी नित्ययुक्त एकभक्तिर्विशिष्यते ।
प्रियो हि ज्ञानिनोऽत्यर्थमहं स च मम प्रियः ॥ १७

उदाराः सर्व एवैते ज्ञानी त्वात्मैव मे मतम् ।
आस्थितः स हि युक्तात्मा मामेवानुत्तमां गतिम् ॥ १८

बहूनां जन्मनामन्ते ज्ञानवान्मां प्रपद्यते ।
वासुदेवः सर्वमिति स महात्मा सुदुर्लभः ॥ १९

कामैस्तैस्तैर्हृतज्ञानाः प्रपद्यन्तेऽन्यदेवताः ।
तं तं नियममास्थाय प्रकृत्या नियताः स्वया ॥ २०

यो यो यां यां तनुं भक्तः श्रद्धयार्चितुमिच्छति ।
तस्य तस्याचलां श्रद्धां तामेव विदधाम्यहम् ॥ २१

स तया श्रद्धया युक्तस्तस्या राधनमीहते ।
लभते च ततः कामान्मयैव विहितान्हि तान् ॥ २२

अन्तवत्तु फलं तेषां तद्भवत्यल्पमेधसाम् ।
देवान्देवयजो यान्ति मद्भक्ता यान्ति मामपि ॥ २३

अव्यक्तं व्यक्तिमापन्नं मन्यन्ते मामबुद्धयः ।
परं भावमजानन्तो ममाव्ययमनुत्तमम् ॥ २४

नाहं प्रकाशः सर्वस्य योगमायासमावृतः ।
मूढोऽयं नाभिजानाति लोको मामजमव्ययम् ॥ २५

वेदाहं समतीतानि वर्तमानानि चार्जुन ।
भविष्याणि च भूतानि मां तु वेद न कश्चन ॥ २६

Verily, this Divine Illusion of Phenomenon manifesting itself in the Qualities is difficult to surmount. Only they who devote themselves to Me and to Me alone can accomplish it.

The sinner, the ignorant, the vile, deprived of spiritual perception by the glamour of Illusion, and he who pursues a godless life—none of them shall find Me.

O Arjuna! The righteous who worship Me are grouped by stages: first they who suffer, next they who desire knowledge, then they who thirst after truth, and lastly they who attain wisdom.

Of all these, he who has gained wisdom, who meditates on Me without ceasing, devoting himself only to Me, he is the best; for by the wise man I am exceedingly beloved and the wise man, too, is beloved by Me.

Noble-minded are they all, but the wise man I hold as my own Self; for he, remaining always at peace with Me, makes Me his final goal.

After many lives, at last the wise man realises Me as I am. A man so enlightened that he sees God everywhere is very difficult to find.

They in whom wisdom is obscured by one desire or the other, worship the lesser Powers, practising many rites which vary according to their temperaments.

But whatever the form of worship, if the devotee have faith, then upon his faith in that worship do I set My own seal.

If he worships one form alone with real faith, then shall his desires be fulfilled through that only; for thus have I ordained.

The fruit that comes to men of limited insight is, after all, finite. They who worship the Lower Powers attain them; but those who worship Me come unto Me alone.

The ignorant think of Me, who am the Unmanifested Spirit, as if I were really in human form. They do not understand that My Supreme Nature is changeless and most excellent.

I am not visible to all, for I am enveloped by the illusion of Phenomenon. This deluded world does not know Me as the Unborn and the Imperishable.

I know, O Arjuna, all beings in the past, the present and the future; but they do not know Me.

इच्छाद्वेषसमुत्थेन द्वन्द्वमोहेन भारत ।
सर्वभूतानि संमोहं सर्गे यान्ति परंतप ॥ २७

येषां त्वन्तगतं पापं जनानां पुण्यकर्मणाम् ।
ते द्वन्द्वमोहनिर्मुक्ता भजन्ते मां दृढव्रताः ॥ २८

जरामरणमोक्षाय मामाश्रित्य यतन्ति ये ।
ते ब्रह्म तद्विदुः कृत्स्नमध्यात्मं कर्म चाखिलम् ॥ २९

साधिभूताधिदैवं मां साधियज्ञं च ये विदुः ।
प्रयाणकालेऽपि च मां ते विदुर्युक्तचेतसः ॥ ३०

इति श्रीमद्भगवद्गीतासु सप्तमोऽध्यायः ॥ ७ ॥

O brave Arjuna! Man lives in a fairy world, deceived by the glamour of opposite sensations, infatuated by desire and aversion.

But those who act righteously, in whom sin has been destroyed, who are free from the infatuation of the conflicting emotions, they worship Me with firm resolution.

Those who make Me their refuge, who strive for liberation from decay and death, they realise the Supreme Spirit, which is their own real Self, and in which all action finds its consummation.

Those who see Me in the life of the world, in the universal sacrifice, and as pure Divinity, keeping their minds steady, they live in Me, even in the crucial hour of death."

Thus, in the Holy Book the Bhagavad Gita, one of the Upanishads, in the Science of the Supreme Spirit, in the Art of Self-Knowledge, in the colloquy between the Divine Lord Shri Krishna and the Prince Arjuna, stands the seventh chapter, entitled: Knowledge and Experience.

EIGHT

·ᘛᘚ·

THE LIFE EVERLASTING

अर्जुन उवाच ।
किं तद्ब्रह्म किमध्यात्मं किं कर्म पुरुषोत्तम ।
अधिभूतं च किं प्रोक्तमधिदैवं किमुच्यते ॥ १

अधियज्ञः कथं कोऽत्र देहेऽस्मिन्मधुसूदन ।
प्रयाणकाले च कथं ज्ञेयोऽसि नियतात्मभिः ॥ २

श्रीभगवानुवाच ।
अक्षरं ब्रह्म परमं स्वभावोऽध्यात्ममुच्यते ।
भूतभावोद्भवकरो विसर्गः कर्मसंज्ञितः ॥ ३

अधिभूतं क्षरो भावः पुरुषश्चाधिदैवतम् ।
अधियज्ञोऽहमेवात्र देहे देहभृतां वर ॥ ४

अन्तकाले च मामेव स्मरन्मुक्त्वा कलेवरम् ।
यः प्रयाति स मद्भावं याति नास्त्यत्र संशयः ॥ ५

यं यं वापि स्मरन्भावं त्यजत्यन्ते कलेवरम् ।
तं तमेवैति कौन्तेय सदा तद्भावभावितः ॥ ६

तस्मात्सर्वेषु कालेषु मामनुस्मर युध्य च ।
मय्यर्पितमनोबुद्धिर्मामेवैष्यस्यसंशयः ॥ ७

अभ्यासयोगयुक्तेन चेतसा नान्यगामिना ।
परमं पुरुषं दिव्यं याति पार्थानुचिन्तयन् ॥ ८

कविं पुराणमनुशासितार-
मणोरणीयांसमनुस्मरेद्यः ।
सर्वस्य धातारमचिन्त्यरूप-
मादित्यवर्णं तमसः परस्तात् ॥ ९

प्रयाणकाले मनसाचलेन
भक्त्या युक्तो योगबलेन चैव ।
भ्रुवोर्मध्ये प्राणमावेश्य सम्य-
क्स तं परं पुरुषमुपैति दिव्यम् ॥ १०

"*Arjuna asked:* O Lord of Lords! What is that which men call the Supreme Spirit, what is man's Spiritual Nature, and what is the Law? What is Matter and what is Divinity?

Who is it who rules the spirit of sacrifice in man; and at the time of death how may those who have learned self-control come to the knowledge of Thee?

The Lord Shri Krishna replied: The Supreme Spirit is the Highest Imperishable Self, and Its Nature is spiritual consciousness. The worlds have been created and are supported by an emanation from the Spirit which is called the Law.

Matter consists of the forms that perish; Divinity is the Supreme Self; and He who inspires the spirit of sacrifice in man, O noblest of thy race, is I Myself, Who now stand in human form before thee.

Whosoever at the time of death thinks only of Me, and thinking thus leaves the body and goes forth, assuredly he will know Me.

On whatever sphere of being the mind of a man may be intent at the time of death, thither will he go.

Therefore meditate always on Me, and fight; if thy mind and thy reason be fixed on Me, to Me shalt thou surely come.

He whose mind does not wander, and who is engaged in constant meditation, attains the Supreme Spirit.

Whoso meditates on the Omniscient, the Ancient, more Minute than the atom, yet the Ruler and Upholder of all, Unimaginable, Brilliant like the Sun, Beyond the reach of darkness;

He who leaves the body with mind unmoved and filled with devotion, by the power of his meditation gathering between his eyebrows his whole vital energy, attains the Supreme.

यदक्षरं वेदविदो वदन्ति
    विशन्ति यद्यतयो वीतरागाः ।
यदिच्छन्तो ब्रह्मचर्यं चरन्ति
    तत्ते पदं संग्रहेण प्रवक्ष्ये ॥ ११
सर्वद्वाराणि संयम्य मनो हृदि निरुध्य च ।
मूर्ध्न्याधायात्मनः प्राणमास्थितो योगधारणाम् ॥ १२
ओमित्येकाक्षरं ब्रह्म व्याहरन्मामनुस्मरन् ।
यः प्रयाति त्यजन्देहं स याति परमां गतिम् ॥ १३
अनन्यचेताः सततं यो मां स्मरति नित्यशः ।
तस्याहं सुलभः पार्थ नित्ययुक्तस्य योगिनः ॥ १४
मामुपेत्य पुनर्जन्म दुःखालयमशाश्वतम् ।
नाप्नुवन्ति महात्मानः संसिद्धिं परमां गताः ॥ १५
आ ब्रह्मभुवनाल्लोकाः पुनरावर्तिनोऽर्जुन ।
मामुपेत्य तु कौन्तेय पुनर्जन्म न विद्यते ॥ १६

Now I will speak briefly of the imperishable goal, proclaimed by those versed in the scriptures, which the mystic attains when free from passion, and for which he is content to undergo the vow of continence.

Closing the gates of the body, drawing the forces of his mind into the heart and by the power of meditation concentrating his vital energy in the brain;

Repeating Om, the Symbol of Eternity, holding Me always in remembrance, he who thus leaves his body and goes forth reaches the Spirit Supreme.

To him who thinks constantly of Me, and of nothing else, to such an ever-faithful devotee, O Arjuna, am I ever accessible.

Coming thus unto Me, these great souls go no more to the misery and death of earthly life, for they have gained perfection.

The worlds, with the whole realm of creation, come and go; but, O Arjuna, whoso comes to Me, for him there is no rebirth.

Those who understand the cosmic day and cosmic night know that one day of creation is a thousand cycles, and that the night is of equal length.

At the dawning of that day all objects in manifestation stream forth from the Unmanifest, and when evening falls they are dissolved into It again.

The same multitude of beings, which have lived on earth so often, all are dissolved as the night of the universe approaches, to issue forth anew when morning breaks. Thus is it ordained.

In truth, therefore, there is the Eternal Unmanifest, which is beyond and above the Unmanifest Spirit of Creation, which is never destroyed when all these beings perish.

The wise say that the Unmanifest and Indestructible is the highest goal of all; when once That is reached, there is no return. That is My Blessed Home.

O Arjuna! That Highest God, in Whom all beings abide, and Who pervades the entire universe, is reached only by whole-hearted devotion.

सहस्रयुगपर्यन्तमहर्यद्ब्रह्मणो विदुः ।
रात्रिं युगसहस्रान्तां तेऽहोरात्रविदो जनाः ॥ १७
अव्यक्ताद्व्यक्तयः सर्वाः प्रभवन्त्यहरागमे ।
रात्र्यागमे प्रलीयन्ते तत्रैवाव्यक्तसंज्ञके ॥ १८
भूतग्रामः स एवायं भूत्वा भूत्वा प्रलीयते ।
रात्र्यागमेऽवशः पार्थ प्रभवत्यहरागमे ॥ १९
परस्तस्मात्तु भावोऽन्योऽव्यक्तोऽव्यक्तात्सनातनः ।
यः स सर्वेषु भूतेषु नश्यत्सु न विनश्यति ॥ २०
अव्यक्तोऽक्षर इत्युक्तस्तमाहुः परमां गतिम् ।
यं प्राप्य न निवर्तन्ते तद्धाम परमं मम ॥ २१
पुरुषः स परः पार्थ भक्त्या लभ्यस्त्वनन्यया ।
यस्यान्तःस्थानि भूतानि येन सर्वमिदं ततम् ॥ २२

यत्र काले त्वनावृत्तिमावृत्तिं चैव योगिनः ।
प्रयाता यान्ति तं कालं वक्ष्यामि भरतर्षभ ॥ २३
अग्निज्योतिरहः शुक्लः षण्मासा उत्तरायणम् ।
तत्र प्रयाता गच्छन्ति ब्रह्म ब्रह्मविदो जनाः ॥ २४
धूमो रात्रिस्तथा कृष्णः षण्मासा दक्षिणायनम् ।
तत्र चान्द्रमसं ज्योतियोगी प्राप्य निवर्तते ॥ २५
शुक्लकृष्णे गती ह्येते जगतः शाश्वते मते ।
एकया यात्यनावृत्तिमन्ययावर्तते पुनः ॥ २६
नैते सृती पार्थ जानन्योगी मुह्यति कश्चन ।
तस्मात्सर्वेषु कालेषु योगयुक्तो भवार्जुन ॥ २७
वेदेषु यज्ञेषु तपःसु चैव
    दानेषु यत्पुण्यफलं प्रदिष्टम् ।
अत्येति तत्सर्वमिदं विदित्वा
    योगी परं स्थानमुपैति चाद्यम् ॥ २८

इति श्रीमद्भगवद्गीतासु अष्टमोऽध्यायः ॥ ८ ॥

Now I will tell thee, O Arjuna, of the times at which, if the mystics go forth, they do not return, and at which they go forth only to return.

If knowing the Supreme Spirit the sage goes forth with fire and light, in the daytime, in the fortnight of the waxing moon and in the six months before the Northern summer solstice, he will attain the Supreme.

But if he departs in gloom, at night, during the fortnight of the waning moon and in the six months before the Southern solstice, then he reaches but lunar light and he will be born again.

These bright and dark paths out of the world have always existed. Whoso takes the former, returns not; he who chooses the latter, returns.

O Arjuna! The saint knowing these paths is not confused. Therefore meditate perpetually.

The sage who knows this passes beyond all merit that comes from the study of the scriptures, from sacrifice, from austerities and charity, and reaches the Supreme Primeval Abode."

Thus, in the Holy Book the Bhagavad Gita, one of the Upanishads, in the Science of the Supreme Spirit, in the Art of Self-Knowledge, in the colloquy between the Divine Lord Shri Krishna and the Prince Arjuna, stands the eighth chapter, entitled: The Life Everlasting.

NINE

·९·

THE SCIENCE OF SCIENCES AND
THE MYSTERY OF MYSTERIES

श्रीभगवानुवाच ।
इदं तु ते गुह्यतमं प्रवक्ष्याम्यनसूयवे ।
ज्ञानं विज्ञानसहितं यज्ज्ञात्वा मोक्ष्यसेऽशुभात् ॥ १
राजविद्या राजगुह्यं पवित्रमिदमुत्तमम् ।
प्रत्यक्षावगमं धर्म्यं सुसुखं कर्तुमव्ययम् ॥ २
अश्रद्दधानाः पुरुषा धर्मस्यास्य परंतप ।
अप्राप्य मां निवर्तन्ते मृत्युसंसारवर्त्मनि ॥ ३
मया ततमिदं सर्वं जगदव्यक्तमूर्तिना ।
मत्स्थानि सर्वभूतानि न चाहं तेष्ववस्थितः ॥ ४
न च मत्स्थानि भूतानि पश्य मे योगमैश्वरम् ।
भूतभृन्न च भूतस्थो ममात्मा भूतभावनः ॥ ५
यथाकाशस्थितो नित्यं वायुः सर्वत्रगो महान् ।
तथा सर्वाणि भूतानि मत्स्थानीत्युपधारय ॥ ६

"*Lord Shri Krishna said:* I will now reveal to thee, since thou doubtest not, that profound mysticism, which when followed by experience, shall liberate thee from sin.

This is the Premier Science, the Sovereign Secret, the Purest and Best; intuitional, righteous; and to him who practiseth it pleasant beyond measure.

They who have no faith in this teaching cannot find Me, but remain lost in the purlieus of this perishable world.

The whole world is pervaded by Me, yet My form is not seen. All living things have their being in Me, yet I am not limited by them.

Nevertheless, they do not consciously abide in Me. Such is My Divine Sovereignty that though I, the Supreme Self, am the cause and upholder of all, yet I remain outside.

As the mighty wind, though moving everywhere, has no resting place but space, so have all these beings no home but Me.

सर्वभूतानि कौन्तेय प्रकृतिं यान्ति मामिकाम् ।
कल्पक्षये पुनस्तानि कल्पादौ विसृजाम्यहम् ॥ ७
प्रकृतिं स्वामवष्टभ्य विसृजामि पुनः पुनः ।
भूतग्राममिमं कृत्स्नमवशं प्रकृतेर्वशात् ॥ ८
न च मां तानि कर्माणि निबध्नन्ति धनंजय ।
उदासीनवदासीनमसक्तं तेषु कर्मसु ॥ ९
मयाध्यक्षेण प्रकृतिः सूयते सचराचरम् ।
हेतुनानेन कौन्तेय जगद्विपरिवर्तते ॥ १०
अवजानन्ति मां मूढा मानुषीं तनुमाश्रितम् ।
परं भावमजानन्तो मम भूतमहेश्वरम् ॥ ११
मोघाशा मोघकर्माणो मोघज्ञाना विचेतसः ।
राक्षसीमासुरीं चैव प्रकृतिं मोहिनीं श्रिताः ॥ १२
महात्मानस्तु मां पार्थ दैवीं प्रकृतिमाश्रिताः ।
भजन्त्यनन्यमनसो ज्ञात्वा भूतादिमव्ययम् ॥ १३
सततं कीर्तयन्तो मां यतन्तश्च दृढव्रताः ।
नमस्यन्तश्च मां भक्त्या नित्ययुक्ता उपासते ॥ १४

All beings, O Arjuna, return at the close of every cosmic cycle into the realm of Nature, which is a part of Me, and at the beginning of the next I send them forth again.

With the help of Nature, again and again I pour forth the whole multitude of beings, whether they will or no, for they are ruled by My Will.

But these acts of Mine do not bind Me. I remain outside and unattached.

Under My guidance, Nature produces all things movable and immovable. Thus it is, O Arjuna, that this universe revolves.

Fools disregard Me, seeing Me clad in human form. They know not that in My higher nature I am the Lord-God of all.

Their hopes are vain, their actions worthless, their knowledge futile; they are without sense, deceitful, barbarous and godless.

But the Great Souls, O Arjuna! Filled with My Divine Spirit, they worship Me, they fix their minds on Me and on Me alone, for they know that I am the imperishable Source of being.

Always extolling Me, strenuous, firm in their vows, prostrating themselves before Me, they worship Me continually with concentrated devotion.

Others worship Me with full consciousness as the One, the Manifold, the Omnipresent, the Universal.

I am the Oblation, the Sacrifice and the Worship; I am the Fuel and the Chant, I am the Butter offered to the fire, I am the Fire itself, and I am the Act of offering.

I am the Father of the universe and its Mother; I am its Nourisher and its Grandfather; I am the Knowable and the Pure; I am Om; and I am the Sacred Scriptures.

I am the Goal, the Sustainer, the Lord, the Witness, the Home, the Shelter, the Lover and the Origin; I am Life and Death; I am the Fountain and the Seed Imperishable.

I am the Heat of the Sun. I release and hold back the Rains. I am Death and Immortality; I am Being and Not-Being.

Those who are versed in the scriptures, who drink the mystic Soma-juice and are purified from sin, but who while worshipping Me with sacrifices pray that I will lead them to heaven; they reach the holy world where lives the Controller of the Powers of Nature, and they enjoy the feasts of Paradise.

Yet although they enjoy the spacious glories of Paradise, nevertheless, when their merit is exhausted, they are born again into this world of mortals. They have followed the letter of the scriptures, yet because they have sought but to fulfil their own desires, they must depart and return again and again.

ज्ञानयज्ञेन चाप्यन्ये यजन्तो मामुपासते ।
एकत्वेन पृथक्त्वेन बहुधा विश्वतोमुखम् ॥ १५
अहं क्रतुरहं यज्ञः स्वधाहमहमौषधम् ।
मन्त्रोऽहमहमेवाज्यमहमग्निरहं हुतम् ॥ १६
पिताहमस्य जगतो माता धाता पितामहः ।
वेद्यं पवित्रमोंकार ऋक्साम यजुरेव च ॥ १७
गतिर्भर्ता प्रभुः साक्षी निवासः शरणं सुहृत् ।
प्रभवः प्रलयः स्थानं निधानं बीजमव्ययम् ॥ १८
तपाम्यहमहं वर्षं निगृह्णाम्युत्सृजामि च ।
अमृतं चैव मृत्युश्च सदसच्चाहमर्जुन ॥ १९
त्रैविद्या मां सोमपाः पूतपापा
    यज्ञैरिष्ट्वा स्वर्गतिं प्रार्थयन्ते ।
ते पुण्यमासाद्य सुरेन्द्रलोक-
    मश्नन्ति दिव्यान्दिवि देवभोगान् ॥ २०
ते तं भुक्त्वा स्वर्गलोकं विशालं
    क्षीणे पुण्ये मर्त्यलोकं विशन्ति ।
एवं त्रयीधर्ममनुप्रपन्ना
    गतागतं कामकामा लभन्ते ॥ २१

But if a man will meditate on Me and Me alone, and will worship Me always and everywhere, I will take upon Myself the fulfilment of his aspiration, and I will safeguard whatsoever he shall attain.

Even those who worship the lesser Powers, if they do so with faith, they thereby worship Me, though not in the right way.

I am the willing recipient of sacrifice, and I am its true Lord. But these do not know Me in truth, and so they sink back.

The votaries of the lesser Powers go to them; the devotees of spirits go to them; they who worship the Powers of Darkness, to such Powers shall they go; and so, too, those who worship Me shall come unto Me.

Whatever a man offers to Me, whether it be a leaf, or a flower, or fruit, or water, I accept it, for it is offered with devotion and purity of mind.

Whatever thou doest, whatever thou dost eat, whatever thou dost sacrifice and give, whatever austerities thou practisest, do all as an offering to Me.

So shall thy action be attended by no result, either good or bad; but through the spirit of renunciation thou shalt come to Me and be free.

अनन्याश्चिन्तयन्तो मां ये जनाः पर्युपासते ।
तेषां नित्याभियुक्तानां योगक्षेमं वहाम्यहम् ॥ २२
येऽप्यन्यदेवता भक्ता यजन्ते श्रद्धयान्विताः ।
तेऽपि मामेव कौन्तेय यजन्त्यविधिपूर्वकम् ॥ २३
अहं हि सर्वयज्ञानां भोक्ता च प्रभुरेव च ।
न तु मामभिजानन्ति तत्त्वेनातश्च्यवन्ति ते ॥ २४
यान्ति देवव्रता देवान्पितॄन्यान्ति पितृव्रताः ।
भूतानि यान्ति भूतेज्या यान्ति मद्याजिनोऽपि माम् ॥ २५
पत्रं पुष्पं फलं तोयं यो मे भक्त्या प्रयच्छति ।
तदहं भक्त्युपहृतमश्नामि प्रयतात्मनः ॥ २६
यत्करोषि यदश्नासि यज्जुहोषि ददासि यत् ।
यत्तपस्यसि कौन्तेय तत्कुरुष्व मदर्पणम् ॥ २७
शुभाशुभफलैरेवं मोक्ष्यसे कर्मबन्धनैः ।
संन्यासयोगयुक्तात्मा विमुक्तो मामुपैष्यसि ॥ २८

90

समोऽहं सर्वभूतेषु न मे द्वेष्योऽस्ति न प्रियः ।
ये भजन्ति तु मां भक्त्या मयि ते तेषु चाप्यहम् ॥ २९
अपि चेत्सुदुराचारो भजते मामनन्यभाक् ।
साधुरेव स मन्तव्यः सम्यग्व्यवसितो हि सः ॥ ३०
क्षिप्रं भवति धर्मात्मा शश्वच्छान्तिं निगच्छति ।
कौन्तेय प्रतिजानीहि न मे भक्तः प्रणश्यति ॥ ३१
मां हि पार्थ व्यपाश्रित्य येऽपि स्युः पापयोनयः ।
स्त्रियो वैश्यास्तथा शूद्रास्तेऽपि यान्ति परां गतिम् ॥ ३२
किं पुनर्ब्राह्मणाः पुण्या भक्ता राजर्षयस्तथा ।
अनित्यमसुखं लोकमिमं प्राप्य भजस्व माम् ॥ ३३
मन्मना भव मद्भक्तो मद्याजी मां नमस्कुरु ।
मामेवैष्यसि युक्त्वैवमात्मानं मत्परायणः ॥ ३४

इति श्रीमद्भगवद्गीतासु नवमोऽध्यायः ॥ ९ ॥

I am the same to all beings. I favour none, and I hate none. But those who worship Me devotedly, they live in Me, and I in them.

Even the most sinful, if he worship Me with his whole heart, shall be considered righteous, for he is treading the right path.

He shall attain spirituality ere long, and Eternal Peace shall be his. O Arjuna! Believe me, My devotee is never lost.

For even the children of sinful parents, and those miscalled the weaker sex, and merchants, and labourers, if only they will make Me their refuge, they shall attain the Highest.

What need then to mention the holy Ministers of God, the devotees and the saintly rulers? Do thou, therefore, born in this changing and miserable world, do thou too worship Me.

Fix thy mind on Me, devote thyself to Me, sacrifice for Me, surrender to Me, make Me the object of thy aspirations, and thou shalt assuredly become one with Me, Who am thine own Self."

Thus, in the Holy Book the Bhagavad Gita, one of the Upanishads, in the Science of the Supreme Spirit, in the Art of Self-Knowledge, in the colloquy between the Divine Lord Shri Krishna and the Prince Arjuna, stands the ninth chapter, entitled:
The Science of Sciences and the Mystery of Mysteries.

TEN

·૬૦·

THE DIVINE MANIFESTATIONS

श्रीभगवानुवाच ।
भूय एव महाबाहो श्रृणु मे परमं वचः ।
यत्तेऽहं प्रीयमाणाय वक्ष्यामि हितकाम्यया ॥ १
न मे विदुः सुरगणाः प्रभवं न महर्षयः ।
अहमादिर्हि देवानां महर्षीणां च सर्वशः ॥ २
यो मामजमनादिं च वेत्ति लोकमहेश्वरम् ।
असंमूढः स मर्त्येषु सर्वपापैः प्रमुच्यते ॥ ३
बुद्धिर्ज्ञानमसंमोहः क्षमा सत्यं दमः शमः ।
सुखं दुःखं भवोऽभावो भयं चाभयमेव च ॥ ४
अहिंसा समता तुष्टिस्तपो दानं यशोऽयशः ।
भवन्ति भावा भूतानां मत्त एव पृथग्विधाः ॥ ५
महर्षयः सप्त पूर्वे चत्वारो मनवस्तथा ।
मद्भावा मानसा जाता येषां लोक इमाः प्रजाः ॥ ६
एतां विभूतिं योगं च मम यो वेत्ति तत्त्वतः ।
सोऽविकम्पेन योगेन युज्यते नात्र संशयः ॥ ७
अहं सर्वस्य प्रभवो मत्तः सर्वं प्रवर्तते ।
इति मत्वा भजन्ते मां बुधा भावसमन्विताः ॥ ८
मच्चित्ता मद्गतप्राणा बोधयन्तः परस्परम् ।
कथयन्तश्च मां नित्यं तुष्यन्ति च रमन्ति च ॥ ९
तेषां सततयुक्तानां भजतां प्रीतिपूर्वकम् ।
ददामि बुद्धियोगं तं येन मामुपयान्ति ते ॥ १०
तेषामेवानुकम्पार्थमहमज्ञानजं तमः ।
नाशयाम्यात्मभावस्थो ज्ञानदीपेन भास्वता ॥ ११

"Lord Shri Krishna said: Now, O Prince! Listen to My supreme advice, which I give thee for the sake of thy welfare, for thou art My beloved.

Neither the professors of divinity nor the great ascetics know My origin, for I am the source of them all.

He who knows Me as the unborn, without beginning, the Lord of the universe, he, stripped of his delusions, becomes free from all conceivable sin.

Intelligence, wisdom, non-illusion, forgiveness, truth, self-control, calmness, pleasure, pain, birth, death, fear and fearlessness;

Harmlessness, equanimity, contentment, austerity, beneficence, fame and failure, all these, the characteristics of beings, spring from Me only.

The seven Great Seers,[*] the Progenitors of mankind, the Ancient Four,[†] and the Lawgivers were born of My Will and came forth direct from Me. The race of mankind has sprung from them.

He who rightly understands My manifested glory and My Creative Power, beyond doubt attains perfect Peace.

I am the source of all; from Me everything flows. Therefore the wise worship Me with unchanging devotion.

With minds concentrated on Me, with lives absorbed in Me, and enlightening each other, they ever feel content and happy.

To those who are always devout and who worship Me with love, I give the power of discrimination, which leads them to Me.

By My grace, I live in their hearts; and I dispel the darkness of ignorance by the shining light of wisdom.

---

[*]Mareechi, Atri, Angira, Pulah, Kratu, Pulastya, Vashishtha.
[†]The Masters: Sanak, Sanandan, Sanatan, Sanatkumar.

Arjuna asked: Thou art the Supreme Spirit, the Eternal Home, the Holiest of the Holy, the Eternal Divine Self, the Primal God, the Unborn and the Omnipresent.

So have said the seers and the divine sage Narada; as well as Asita, Devala and Vyasa; and Thou Thyself also sayest it.

I believe in what Thou hast said, my Lord! For neither the godly nor the godless comprehend Thy manifestation.

Thou alone knowest Thyself, by the power of Thy Self; Thou the Supreme Spirit, the Source and Master of all being, the Lord of Lords, the Ruler of the Universe.

Please tell me all about Thy glorious manifestations, by means of which Thou pervadest the world.

O Master! How shall I, by constant meditation, know Thee? My Lord! What are Thy various manifestations through which I am to meditate on Thee?

Tell me again, I pray, about the fullness of Thy power and Thy glory; for I feel that I am never satisfied when I listen to Thy immortal words.

अर्जुन उवाच ।
परं ब्रह्म परं धाम पवित्रं परमं भवान् ।
पुरुषं शाश्वतं दिव्यमादिदेवमजं विभुम् ॥ १२
आहुस्त्वामृषयः सर्वे देवर्षिर्नारदस्तथा ।
असितो देवलो व्यासः स्वयं चैव ब्रवीषि मे ॥ १३
सर्वमेतदृतं मन्ये यन्मां वदसि केशव ।
न हि ते भगवन्व्यक्तिं विदुर्देवा न दानवाः ॥ १४
स्वयमेवात्मनात्मानं वेत्थ त्वं पुरुषोत्तम ।
भूतभावन भूतेश देवदेव जगत्पते ॥ १५
वक्तुमर्हस्यशेषेण दिव्या ह्यात्मविभूतयः ।
याभिर्विभूतिभिर्लोकानिमांस्त्वं व्याप्य तिष्ठसि ॥ १६
कथं विद्यामहं योगिंस्त्वां सदा परिचिन्तयन् ।
केषु केषु च भावेषु चिन्त्योऽसि भगवन्मया ॥ १७
विस्तरेणात्मनो योगं विभूतिं च जनार्दन ।
भूयः कथय तृप्तिर्हि शृण्वतो नास्ति मेऽमृतम् ॥ १८

Lord Shri Krishna replied: So be it, My beloved friend! I will unfold to thee some of the chief aspects of My glory. Of its full extent there is no end.

O Arjuna! I am the Self, seated in the hearts of all beings; I am the beginning and the life, and I am the end of them all.

Of all creative Powers I am the Creator, of luminaries the Sun; the Whirlwind among the winds, and the Moon among planets.

Of the Vedas I am the Hymns, I am the Electric Force in the Powers of Nature; of the senses I am the Mind; and I am the Intelligence in all that lives.

Among Forces of Vitality I am the Life, I am Mammon to the heathen and the godless; I am the Energy in fire, earth, wind, sky, heaven, sun, moon and planets; and among mountains I am the Mount Meru.

श्रीभगवानुवाच ।
हन्त ते कथयिष्यामि दिव्या ह्यात्मविभूतयः ।
प्राधान्यतः कुरुश्रेष्ठ नास्त्यन्तो विस्तरस्य मे ॥ १९
अहमात्मा गुडाकेश सर्वभूताशयस्थितः ।
अहमादिश्च मध्यं च भूतानामन्त एव च ॥ २०
आदित्यानामहं विष्णुर्ज्योतिषां रविरंशुमान् ।
मरीचिर्मरुतामस्मि नक्षत्राणामहं शशी ॥ २१
वेदानां सामवेदोऽस्मि देवानामस्मि वासवः ।
इन्द्रियाणां मनश्चास्मि भूतानामस्मि चेतना ॥ २२
रुद्राणां शंकरश्चास्मि वित्तेशो यक्षरक्षसाम् ।
वसूनां पावकश्चास्मि मेरुः शिखरिणामहम् ॥ २३

पुरोधसां च मुख्यं मां विद्धि पार्थ बृहस्पतिम् ।
सेनानीनामहं स्कन्दः सरसामस्मि सागरः ॥ २४
महर्षीणां भृगुरहं गिरामस्म्येकमक्षरम् ।
यज्ञानां जपयज्ञोऽस्मि स्थावराणां हिमालयः ॥ २५
अश्वत्थः सर्ववृक्षाणां देवर्षीणां च नारदः ।
गन्धर्वाणां चित्ररथः सिद्धानां कपिलो मुनिः ॥ २६
उच्चैःश्रवसमश्वानां विद्धि माममृतोद्भवम् ।
ऐरावतं गजेन्द्राणां नराणां च नराधिपम् ॥ २७
आयुधानामहं वज्रं धेनूनामस्मि कामधुक् ।
प्रजनश्चास्मि कन्दर्पः सर्पाणामस्मि वासुकिः ॥ २८
अनन्तश्चास्मि नागानां वरुणो यादसामहम् ।
पितॄणामर्यमा चास्मि यमः संयमतामहम् ॥ २९
प्रह्लादश्चास्मि दैत्यानां कालः कलयतामहम् ।
मृगाणां च मृगेन्द्रोऽहं वैनतेयश्च पक्षिणाम् ॥ ३०
पवनः पवतामस्मि रामः शस्त्रभृतामहम् ।
झषाणां मकरश्चास्मि स्रोतसामस्मि जाह्नवी ॥ ३१
सर्गाणामादिरन्तश्च मध्यं चैवाहमर्जुन ।
अध्यात्मविद्या विद्यानां वादः प्रवदतामहम् ॥ ३२
अक्षराणामकारोऽस्मि द्वन्द्वः सामासिकस्य च ।
अहमेवाक्षयः कालो धाताहं विश्वतोमुखः ॥ ३३
मृत्युः सर्वहरश्चाहमुद्भवश्च भविष्यताम् ।
कीर्तिः श्रीर्वाक्च नारीणां स्मृतिर्मेधा धृतिः क्षमा ॥ ३४
बृहत्साम तथा साम्नां गायत्री छन्दसामहम् ।
मासानां मार्गशीर्षोऽहमृतूनां कुसुमाकरः ॥ ३५
द्यूतं छलयतामस्मि तेजस्तेजस्विनामहम् ।
जयोऽस्मि व्यवसायोऽस्मि सत्त्वं सत्त्ववतामहम् ॥ ३६

Among the priests, know, O Arjuna, that I am the Apostle Brihaspati; of generals I am Skanda, the Commander-in-Chief, and of waters I am the Ocean.

Of the great seers I am Bhrigu, of words I am Om, of offerings I am the silent prayer, among things immovable I am the Himalayas.

Of trees I am the sacred Fig-tree, of the Divine Seers Narada, of the heavenly singers I am Chitraratha, their Leader, and of sages I am Kapila.

Know that among horses I am Pegasus, the heaven-born; among the lordly elephants I am the White one, and I am the Ruler among men.

I am the Thunderbolt among weapons; of cows I am the Cow of Plenty, I am Passion in those who procreate, and I am the Cobra among serpents.

I am the King-python among snakes, I am the Aqueous Principle among those that live in water, I am the Father of fathers, and among rulers I am Death.

And I am the devotee Prahlad among the heathen; of Time I am the Eternal Present; I am the Lion among beasts and the Eagle among birds.

I am the Wind among the purifiers, the King Rama among warriors; I am the Crocodile among the fishes, and I am the Ganges among the rivers.

I am the Beginning, the Middle and the End in creation; among sciences, I am the science of Spirituality; I am the Discussion among disputants.

Of letters I am A; I am the copulative in compound words; I am Time inexhaustible; and I am the all-pervading Preserver.

I am all-devouring Death; I am the Origin of all that shall happen; I am Fame, Fortune, Speech, Memory, Intellect, Constancy and Forgiveness.

Of hymns I am Brihatsama, of metres I am Gayatri, among the months I am Margasheersha (December), and I am the Spring among seasons.

I am the Gambling of the cheat and the Splendour of the splendid; I am Victory; I am Effort; and I am the Purity of the pure.

I am Shri Krishna among the Vrishni-clan and Arjuna among the Pandavas; of the saints I am Vyasa, and I am the Shukracharya among the sages.

I am the Sceptre of rulers, the Strategy of the conquerors, the Silence of mystery, the Wisdom of the wise.

I am the Seed of all being, O Arjuna! No creature moving or unmoving can live without Me.

O Arjuna! The aspects of My divine life are endless. I have mentioned but a few by way of illustration.

Whatever is glorious, excellent, beautiful and mighty, be assured that it comes from a fragment of My splendour.

But what is the use of all these details to thee? O Arjuna! I sustain this universe with only a small part of Myself."

Thus, in the Holy Book the Bhagavad Gita, one of the Upanishads, in the Science of the Supreme Spirit, in the Art of Self-Knowledge, in the colloquy between the Divine Lord Shri Krishna and the Prince Arjuna, stands the tenth chapter, entitled: The Divine Manifestations.

वृष्णीनां वासुदेवोऽस्मि पाण्डवानां धनंजयः ।
मुनीनामप्यहं व्यासः कवीनामुशना कविः ॥ ३७

दण्डो दमयतामस्मि नीतिरस्मि जिगीषताम् ।
मौनं चैवास्मि गुह्यानां ज्ञानं ज्ञानवतामहम् ॥ ३८

यच्चापि सर्वभूतानां बीजं तदहमर्जुन ।
न तदस्ति विना यत्स्यान्मया भूतं चराचरम् ॥ ३९

नान्तोऽस्ति मम दिव्यानां विभूतीनां परंतप ।
एष तूद्देशतः प्रोक्तो विभूतेर्विस्तरो मया ॥ ४०

यद्यद्विभूतिमत्सत्त्वं श्रीमदूर्जितमेव वा ।
तत्तदेवावगच्छ त्वं मम तेजोंऽशसंभवम् ॥ ४१

अथ वा बहुनैतेन किं ज्ञातेन तवार्जुन ।
विष्टभ्याहमिदं कृत्स्नमेकांशेन स्थितो जगत् ॥ ४२

इति श्रीमद्भगवद्गीतासु दशमोऽध्यायः ॥ १० ॥

ELEVEN

·♀♀·

THE COSMIC VISION

"*Arjuna said:* My Lord! Thy words concerning the Supreme Secret of Self, given for my blessing, have dispelled the illusions which surrounded me.

O Lord, whose eyes are like the lotus petal! Thou hast described in detail the origin and the dissolution of being, and Thine own Eternal Majesty.

I believe all as Thou hast declared it. I long now to have a vision of Thy Divine Form, O Thou Most High!

If Thou thinkest that it can be made possible for me to see it, show me, O Lord of Lords, Thine own Eternal Self!

Lord Shri Krishna replied: Behold, O Arjuna! My celestial forms, by hundreds and thousands, various in kind, in colour and in shape.

Behold thou the Powers of Nature: fire, earth, wind and sky; the sun, the heavens, the moon, the stars; all the forces of vitality and of healing; and the roving winds. See the myriad wonders revealed to none but thee.

Here, in Me living as one, O Arjuna, behold the whole universe, movable and immovable, and anything else that thou wouldst see!

Yet since with mortal eyes thou canst not see Me, lo! I give thee the Divine Sight. See now the glory of My Sovereignty."

अर्जुन उवाच ।
मदनुग्रहाय परमं गुह्यमध्यात्मसंज्ञितम् ।
यत्त्वयोक्तं वचस्तेन मोहोऽयं विगतो मम ॥ १
भवाप्ययौ हि भूतानां श्रुतौ विस्तरशो मया ।
त्वत्तः कमलपत्राक्ष माहात्म्यमपि चाव्ययम् ॥ २
एवमेतद्यथात्थ त्वमात्मानं परमेश्वर ।
द्रष्टुमिच्छामि ते रूपमैश्वरं पुरुषोत्तम ॥ ३
मन्यसे यदि तच्छक्यं मया द्रष्टुमिति प्रभो ।
योगेश्वर ततो मे त्वं दर्शयात्मानमव्ययम् ॥ ४
श्रीभगवानुवाच ।
पश्य मे पार्थ रूपाणि शतशोऽथ सहस्रशः ।
नानाविधानि दिव्यानि नानावर्णाकृतीनि च ॥ ५
पश्यादित्यान्वसून्रुद्रानश्विनौ मरुतस्तथा ।
बहून्यदृष्टपूर्वाणि पश्याश्चर्याणि भारत ॥ ६
इहैकस्थं जगत्कृत्स्नं पश्याद्य सचराचरम् ।
मम देहे गुडाकेश यच्चान्यद्द्रष्टुमिच्छसि ॥ ७
न तु मां शक्यसे द्रष्टुमनेनैव स्वचक्षुषा ।
दिव्यं ददामि ते चक्षुः पश्य मे योगमैश्वरम् ॥ ८

Sanjaya continued: "*Having thus spoken, O King, the Lord Shri Krishna, the Almighty Prince of Wisdom, showed to Arjuna the Supreme Form of the Great God.*

There were countless eyes and mouths, and mystic forms innumerable, with shining ornaments and flaming celestial weapons.

Crowned with heavenly garlands, clothed in shining garments, anointed with divine unctions, He showed Himself as the Resplendent One, Marvellous, Boundless, Omnipresent.

Could a thousand suns blaze forth together it would be but a faint reflection of the radiance of the Lord-God.

In that vision Arjuna saw the universe, with its manifold shapes, all embraced in One, its Supreme Lord.

Thereupon Arjuna, dumb with awe, his hair on end, his head bowed, his hands clasped in salutation, addressed the Lord thus:

Arjuna said: O Almighty God! I see in Thee the powers of Nature, the various creatures of the world, the Progenitor on his lotus throne, the Sages and the shining angels.

I see Thee, infinite in form, with, as it were, faces, eyes and limbs everywhere; no beginning, no middle, no end; O Thou Lord of the Universe, Whose Form is universal!

I see Thee with the crown, the sceptre and the discus; a blaze of splendour. Scarce can I gaze on thee, so radiant Thou art, glowing like the blazing fire, brilliant as the sun, immeasurable.

संजय उवाच ।

एवमुक्त्वा ततो राजन्महायोगेश्वरो हरिः ।
दर्शयामास पार्थाय परमं रूपमैश्वरम् ॥ ९

अनेकवक्त्रनयनमनेकाद्भुतदर्शनम् ।
अनेकदिव्याभरणं दिव्यानेकोद्यतायुधम् ॥ १०

दिव्यमाल्याम्बरधरं दिव्यगन्धानुलेपनम् ।
सर्वाश्चर्यमयं देवमनन्तं विश्वतोमुखम् ॥ ११

दिवि सूर्यसहस्रस्य भवेद्युगपदुत्थिता ।
यदि भाः सदृशी सा स्याद्भासस्तस्य महात्मनः ॥ १२

तत्रैकस्थं जगत्कृत्स्नं प्रविभक्तमनेकधा ।
अपश्यद्देवदेवस्य शरीरे पाण्डवस्तदा ॥ १३

ततः स विस्मयाविष्टो हृष्टरोमा धनंजयः ।
प्रणम्य शिरसा देवं कृताञ्जलिरभाषत ॥ १४

अर्जुन उवाच ।

पश्यामि देवांस्तव देव देहे
सर्वांस्तथा भूतविशेषसंघान् ।
ब्रह्माणमीशं कमलासनस्थ-
मृषींश्च सर्वानुरगांश्च दिव्यान् ॥ १५

अनेकबाहूदरवक्त्रनेत्रं
पश्यामि त्वा सर्वतोऽनन्तरूपम् ।
नान्तं न मध्यं न पुनस्तवादिं
पश्यामि विश्वेश्वर विश्वरूप ॥ १६

किरीटिनं गदिनं चक्रिणं च
तेजोराशिं सर्वतो दीप्तिमन्तम् ।
पश्यामि त्वां दुर्निरीक्ष्यं समन्ता-
द्दीप्तानलार्कद्युतिमप्रमेयम् ॥ १७

Imperishable art Thou, the Sole One worthy to be known, the priceless Treasure-house of the universe, the immortal Guardian of the Life Eternal, the Spirit Everlasting.

Without beginning, without middle and without end, infinite in power, Thine arms all-embracing, the sun and moon Thine eyes, Thy face beaming with the fire of sacrifice, flooding the whole universe with light.

Alone Thou fillest all the quarters of the sky, earth and heaven, and the regions between. O Almighty Lord! Seeing Thy marvellous and awe-inspiring Form, the spheres tremble with fear.

The troops of celestial Beings enter into Thee, some invoking Thee in fear, with folded palms; the Great Seers and Adepts sing hymns to Thy Glory, saying 'All Hail.'

The Vital Forces, the Major stars, Fire, Earth, Air, Sky, Sun, Heaven, Moon and Planets; the Angels, the Guardians of the Universe, the divine Healers, the Winds, the Fathers, the Heavenly Singers; and hosts of Mammon-worshippers, demons as well as saints, are amazed.

Seeing Thy stupendous Form, O Most Mighty, with its myriad faces, its innumerable eyes and limbs and terrible jaws, I myself and all the worlds are overwhelmed with awe.

When I see Thee, touching the Heavens, glowing with colour, with open mouth and wide open fiery eyes, I am terrified. O my Lord! My courage and my peace of mind desert me.

When I see Thy mouths with their fearful jaws like glowing fires at the dissolution of creation, I lose all sense of place; I find no rest. Be merciful, O Lord in whom this universe abides!

त्वमक्षरं परमं वेदितव्यं
    त्वमस्य विश्वस्य परं निधानम् ।
त्वमव्ययः शाश्वतधर्मगोप्ता
    सनातनस्त्वं पुरुषो मतो मे ॥ १८

अनादिमध्यान्तमनन्तवीर्य-
    मनन्तबाहुं शशिसूर्यनेत्रम् ।
पश्यामि त्वां दीप्तहुताशवक्त्रं
    स्वतेजसा विश्वमिदं तपन्तम् ॥ १९

द्यावापृथिव्योरिदमन्तरं हि
    व्याप्तं त्वयैकेन दिशश्च सर्वाः ।
दृष्ट्वाद्भुतं रूपमिदं तवोग्रं
    लोकत्रयं प्रव्यथितं महात्मन् ॥ २०

अमी हि त्वा सुरसंघा विशन्ति
    केचिद्भीताः प्राञ्जलयो गृणन्ति ।
स्वस्तीत्युक्त्वा महर्षिसिद्धसंघाः
    स्तुवन्ति त्वां स्तुतिभिः पुष्कलाभिः ॥ २१

रुद्रादित्या वसवो ये च साध्या
    विश्वेऽश्विनौ मरुतश्चोष्मपाश्च ।
गन्धर्वयक्षासुरसिद्धसंघा
    वीक्षन्ते त्वा विस्मिताश्चैव सर्वे ॥ २२

रूपं महत्ते बहुवक्त्रनेत्रं
    महाबाहो बहुबाहूरुपादम् ।
बहूदरं बहुदंष्ट्राकरालं
    दृष्ट्वा लोकाः प्रव्यथितास्तथाहम् ॥ २३

नभःस्पृशं दीप्तमनेकवर्णं
    व्यात्ताननं दीप्तविशालनेत्रम् ।
दृष्ट्वा हि त्वां प्रव्यथितान्तरात्मा
    धृतिं न विन्दामि शमं च विष्णो ॥ २४

दंष्ट्राकरालानि च ते मुखानि
    दृष्ट्वैव कालानलसंनिभानि ।
दिशो न जाने न लभे च शर्म
    प्रसीद देवेश जगन्निवास ॥ २५

अमी च त्वां धृतराष्ट्रस्य पुत्राः
    सर्वे सहैवावनिपालसंघैः ।
भीष्मो द्रोणः सूतपुत्रस्तथासौ
    सहास्मदीयैरपि योधमुख्यैः ॥ २६
वक्त्राणि ते त्वरमाणा विशन्ति
    दंष्ट्राकरालानि भयानकानि ।
केचिद्विलग्ना दशनान्तरेषु
    संदृश्यन्ते चूर्णितैरुत्तमाङ्गैः ॥ २७
यथा नदीनां बहवोऽम्बुवेगाः
    समुद्रमेवाभिमुखा द्रवन्ति ।
तथा तवामी नरलोकवीरा
    विशन्ति वक्त्राण्यभिविज्वलन्ति ॥ २८
यथा प्रदीप्तं ज्वलनं पतंगा
    विशन्ति नाशाय समृद्धवेगाः ।
तथैव नाशाय विशन्ति लोका-
    स्तवापि वक्त्राणि समृद्धवेगाः ॥ २९
लेलिह्यसे ग्रसमानः समन्ता-
    ल्लोकान्समग्रान्वदनैर्ज्वलद्भिः ।
तेजोभिरापूर्य जगत्समग्रं
    भासस्तवोग्राः प्रतपन्ति विष्णो ॥ ३०
आख्याहि मे को भवानुग्ररूपो
    नमोऽस्तु ते देववर प्रसीद ।
विज्ञातुमिच्छामि भवन्तमाद्यं
    न हि प्रजानामि तव प्रवृत्तिम् ॥ ३१
    श्रीभगवानुवाच ।
कालोऽस्मि लोकक्षयकृत्प्रवृद्धो
    लोकान्समाहर्तुमिह प्रवृत्तः ।
ऋतेऽपि त्वा न भविष्यन्ति सर्वे
    येऽवस्थिताः प्रत्यनीकेषु योधाः ॥ ३२
तस्मात्त्वमुत्तिष्ठ यशो लभस्व
    जित्वा शत्रून्भुङ्क्ष्व राज्यं समृद्धम् ।
मयैवैते निहताः पूर्वमेव
    निमित्तमात्रं भव सव्यसाचिन् ॥ ३३
द्रोणं च भीष्मं च जयद्रथं च
    कर्णं तथान्यानपि योधवीरान् ।
मया हतांस्त्वं जहि मा व्यथिष्ठा
    युध्यस्व जेतासि रणे सपत्नान् ॥ ३४

All these sons of Dhritarashtra, with the hosts of princes, Bheeshma, Drona and Karna, as well as the other warrior chiefs belonging to our side;

I see them all rushing headlong into Thy mouths, with terrible tusks, horrible to behold. Some are mangled between Thy jaws, with their heads crushed to atoms.

As rivers in flood surge furiously to the ocean, so these heroes, the greatest among men, fling themselves into Thy flaming mouths.

As moths fly impetuously to the flame only to be killed, so these men rush into Thy mouths to court their own destruction.

Thou seemest to swallow up the worlds, to lap them in flame. Thy glory fills the universe. Thy fierce rays beat down upon it irresistibly.

Tell me then who Thou art, that wearest this dreadful Form? I bow before Thee, O Mighty One! Have mercy, I pray, and let me see Thee as Thou wert at first. I do not know what Thou intendest.

Lord Shri Krishna replied: I have shown myself to thee as the Destroyer who lays waste the world and whose purpose now is destruction. In spite of thy efforts, all these warriors gathered for battle shall not escape death.

Then gird up thy loins and conquer. Subdue thy foes and enjoy the kingdom in prosperity. I have already doomed them. Be thou my instrument, Arjuna!

Drona and Bheeshma, Jayadratha and Karna, and other brave warriors—I have condemned them all. Destroy them; fight and fear not. Thy foes shall be crushed."

Sanjaya continued: "Having heard these words from the Lord Shri Krishna, the Prince Arjuna, with folded hands trembling, prostrated himself and with choking voice, bowing down again and again, and overwhelmed with awe, once more addressed the Lord.

Arjuna said: My Lord! It is natural that the world revels and rejoices when it sings the praises of Thy glory; the demons fly in fear and the saints offer Thee their salutations.

How should they do otherwise? O Thou Supremest Self, greater than the Powers of creation, the First Cause, Infinite, the Lord of Lords, the Home of the universe, Imperishable, Being and Not-Being, yet transcending both.

Thou art the Primal God, the Ancient, the Supreme Abode of this universe, the Knower, the Knowledge and the Final Home. Thou fillest everything. Thy form is infinite.

Thou art the Wind, Thou art Death, Thou art the Fire, the Water, the Moon, the Father and the Grandfather. Honour and glory to Thee a thousand and a thousand times! Again and again, salutation be to Thee, O my Lord!

Salutations to Thee in front and on every side, Thou who encompasseth me round about. Thy power is infinite; Thy majesty immeasurable; Thou upholdest all things; yea, Thou Thyself art All.

संजय उवाच ।
एतच्छ्रुत्वा वचनं केशवस्य
    कृताञ्जलिर्वेपमानः किरीटी ।
नमस्कृत्वा भूय एवाह कृष्णं
    सगद्गदं भीतभीतः प्रणम्य ॥ ३५

अर्जुन उवाच ।
स्थाने हृषीकेश तव प्रकीर्त्या
    जगत्प्रहृष्यत्यनुरज्यते च ।
रक्षांसि भीतानि दिशो द्रवन्ति
    सर्वे नमस्यन्ति च सिद्धसंघाः ॥ ३६

कस्माच्च ते न नमेरन्महात्म-
    न्गरीयसे ब्रह्मणोऽप्यादिकर्त्रे ।
अनन्त देवेश जगन्निवास
    त्वमक्षरं सदसत्तत्परं यत् ॥ ३७

त्वमादिदेवः पुरुषः पुराण-
    स्त्वमस्य विश्वस्य परं निधानम् ।
वेत्तासि वेद्यं च परं च धाम
    त्वया ततं विश्वमनन्तरूप ॥ ३८

वायुर्यमोऽग्निर्वरुणः शशाङ्कः
    प्रजापतिस्त्वं प्रपितामहश्च ।
नमो नमस्तेऽस्तु सहस्रकृत्वः
    पुनश्च भूयोऽपि नमो नमस्ते ॥ ३९

नमः पुरस्तादथ पृष्ठतस्ते
    नमोऽस्तु ते सर्वत एव सर्व ।
अनन्तवीर्यामितविक्रमस्त्वं
    सर्वं समाप्नोषि ततोऽसि सर्वः ॥ ४०

Whatever I have said unto Thee in rashness, taking Thee only for a friend and addressing Thee as 'O Krishna! O Yadava! O Friend!' in thoughtless familiarity, not understanding Thy greatness;

Whatever insult I have offered to Thee in jest, in sport or in repose, in conversation or at the banquet, alone or in a multitude, I ask Thy forgiveness for them all, O Thou Who art without an equal!

For Thou art the Father of all things movable and immovable, the Worshipful, the Master of Masters! In all the worlds there is none equal to Thee, how then superior, O Thou who standeth alone, Supreme.

Therefore I prostrate myself before Thee, O Lord! Most Adorable! I salute Thee, I ask Thy blessing. Only Thou canst be trusted to bear with me, as father to son, as friend to friend, as lover to his beloved.

I rejoice that I have seen what never man saw before; yet, O Lord! I am overwhelmed with fear. Please take again the Form I know. Be merciful, O Lord! Thou Who art the Home of the whole universe.

I long to see Thee as Thou wert before, with the crown, the sceptre and the discus in Thy hands; in Thy other Form, with Thy four hands, O Thou Whose arms are countless and Whose forms are infinite.

Lord Shri Krishna replied: My beloved friend! It is only through My grace and power that thou hast been able to see this vision of splendour, the Universal, the Infinite, the Original. Never has it been seen by any but thee.

Not by study of the scriptures, not by sacrifice or gift, not by ritual or rigorous austerity, is it possible for man on earth to see what thou hast seen, O thou foremost hero of the Kuru-clan!

Be not afraid or bewildered by the terrible vision. Put away thy fear and, with joyful mind, see Me once again in My usual Form."

सखेति मत्वा प्रसभं यदुक्तं
　　हे कृष्ण हे यादव हे सखेति ।
अजानता महिमानं तवेदं
　　मया प्रमादात्प्रणयेन वापि ॥ ४१
यच्चावहासार्थमसत्कृतोऽसि
　　विहारशय्यासनभोजनेषु ।
एकोऽथ वाप्यच्युत तत्समक्षं
　　तत्क्षामये त्वामहमप्रमेयम् ॥ ४२
पितासि लोकस्य चराचरस्य
　　त्वमस्य पूज्यश्च गुरुर्गरीयान् ।
न त्वत्समोऽस्त्यभ्यधिकः कुतोऽन्यो
　　लोकत्रयेऽप्यप्रतिमप्रभाव ॥ ४३
तस्मात्प्रणम्य प्रणिधाय कायं
　　प्रसादये त्वामहमीशमीड्यम् ।
पितेव पुत्रस्य सखेव सख्युः
　　प्रियः प्रियायार्हसि देव सोढुम् ॥ ४४
अदृष्टपूर्वं हृषितोऽस्मि दृष्ट्वा
　　भयेन च प्रव्यथितं मनो मे ।
तदेव मे दर्शय देव रूपं
　　प्रसीद देवेश जगन्निवास ॥ ४५
किरीटिनं गदिनं चक्रहस्त-
　　मिच्छामि त्वां द्रष्टुमहं तथैव ।
तेनैव रूपेण चतुर्भुजेन
　　सहस्रबाहो भव विश्वमूर्ते ॥ ४६
श्रीभगवानुवाच ।
मया प्रसन्नेन तवार्जुनेदं
　　रूपं परं दर्शितमात्मयोगात् ।
तेजोमयं विश्वमनन्तमाद्यं
　　यन्मे त्वदन्येन न दृष्टपूर्वम् ॥ ४७
न वेदयज्ञाध्ययनैर्न दानै-
　　र्न च क्रियाभिर्न तपोभिरुग्रैः ।
एवंरूपः शक्य अहं नृलोके
　　द्रष्टुं त्वदन्येन कुरुप्रवीर ॥ ४८
मा ते व्यथा मा च विमूढभावो
　　दृष्ट्वा रूपं घोरमीदृङ्ममेदम् ।
व्यपेतभीः प्रीतमनाः पुनस्त्वं
　　तदेव मे रूपमिदं प्रपश्य ॥ ४९

संजय उवाच ।
इत्यर्जुनं वासुदेवस्तथोक्त्वा
खकं रूपं दर्शयामास भूयः ।
आश्वासयामास च भीतमेनं
भूत्वा पुनः सौम्यवपुर्महात्मा ॥ ५०
अर्जुन उवाच ।
दृष्ट्वेदं मानुषं रूपं तव सौम्यं जनार्दन ।
इदानीमस्मि संवृत्तः सचेताः प्रकृतिं गतः ॥ ५१
श्रीभगवानुवाच ।
सुदुर्दर्शमिदं रूपं दृष्टवानसि यन्मम ।
देवा अप्यस्य रूपस्य नित्यं दर्शनकाङ्क्षिणः ॥ ५२
नाहं वेदैर्न तपसा न दानेन न चेज्यया ।
शक्य एवंविधो द्रष्टुं दृष्टवानसि मां यथा ॥ ५३
भक्त्या त्वनन्यया शक्य अहमेवंविधोऽर्जुन ।
ज्ञातुं द्रष्टुं च तत्त्वेन प्रवेष्टुं च परंतप ॥ ५४
मत्कर्मकृन्मत्परमो मद्भक्तः सङ्गवर्जितः ।
निर्वैरः सर्वभूतेषु यः स मामेति पाण्डव ॥ ५५

इति श्रीमद्भगवद्गीतासु एकादशोऽध्यायः ॥ ११ ॥

Sanjaya continued: "Having thus spoken to Arjuna, Lord Shri Krishna showed Himself again in His accustomed form; and the Mighty Lord, in gentle tones, softly consoled him who lately trembled with fear.

Arjuna said: Seeing Thee in Thy gentle human form, my Lord, I am myself again, calm once more.

Lord Shri Krishna replied: It is hard to see this vision of Me that thou hast seen. Even the most powerful have longed for it in vain.

Not by study of the scriptures, or by austerities, not by gifts or sacrifices, is it possible to see Me as thou hast done.

Only by tireless devotion can I be seen and known; only thus can a man become one with Me, O Arjuna!

He whose every action is done for My sake, to whom I am the final goal, who loves Me only and hates no one—O My dearest Son, only he can realise Me!"

Thus, in the Holy Book the Bhagavad Gita, one of the Upanishads, in the Science of the Supreme Spirit, in the Art of Self-Knowledge, in the colloquy between the Divine Lord Shri Krishna and the Prince Arjuna, stands the eleventh chapter, entitled: The Cosmic Vision.

TWELVE

·१२·

BHAKTI-YOGA
—THE PATH OF LOVE

"*Arjuna asked:* My Lord! Which are the better devotees who worship Thee, those who try to know Thee as a Personal God, or those who worship Thee as Impersonal and Indestructible?

Lord Shri Krishna replied: Those who keep their minds fixed on Me, who worship Me always with unwavering faith and concentration; these are the very best.

Those who worship Me as the Indestructible, the Undefinable, the Unmanifest, the Omnipresent, the Unthinkable, the Primeval, the Immutable and the Eternal;

Subduing their senses, viewing all conditions of life with the same eye, and working for the welfare of all beings, assuredly they come to Me.

But they who thus fix their attention on the Absolute and Impersonal encounter greater hardships, for it is difficult for those who possess a body to realise Me as without one.

Verily, those who surrender their actions to Me, who muse on Me, worship Me and meditate on Me alone, with no thought save of Me,

O Arjuna! I rescue them quickly from the ocean of life and death, for their minds are fixed on Me.

अर्जुन उवाच ।
एवं सततयुक्ता ये भक्तास्त्वां पर्युपासते ।
ये चाप्यक्षरमव्यक्तं तेषां के योगवित्तमाः ॥ १
श्रीभगवानुवाच ।
मय्यावेश्य मनो ये मां नित्ययुक्ता उपासते ।
श्रद्धया परयोपेतास्ते मे युक्ततमा मताः ॥ २
ये त्वक्षरमनिर्देश्यमव्यक्तं पर्युपासते ।
सर्वत्रगमचिन्त्यं च कूटस्थमचलं ध्रुवम् ॥ ३
संनियम्येन्द्रियग्रामं सर्वत्र समबुद्धयः ।
ते प्राप्नुवन्ति मामेव सर्वभूतहिते रताः ॥ ४
क्लेशोऽधिकतरस्तेषामव्यक्तासक्तचेतसाम् ।
अव्यक्ता हि गतिर्दुःखं देहवद्भिरवाप्यते ॥ ५
ये तु सर्वाणि कर्माणि मयि संन्यस्य मत्पराः ।
अनन्येनैव योगेन मां ध्यायन्त उपासते ॥ ६
तेषामहं समुद्धर्ता मृत्युसंसारसागरात् ।
भवामि नचिरात्पार्थ मय्यावेशितचेतसाम् ॥ ७

118

Then let thy mind cling only to Me, let thy intellect abide in Me; and without doubt thou shalt live hereafter in Me alone.

But if thou canst not fix thy mind firmly on Me, then, My beloved friend, try to do so by constant practice.

And if thou art not strong enough to practise concentration, then devote thyself to My service, do all thine acts for My sake, and thou shalt still attain the goal.

And if thou art too weak even for this, then seek refuge in union with Me, and with perfect self-control renounce the fruit of all thy action.

Knowledge is superior to blind action, meditation to mere knowledge, renunciation of the fruit of action to meditation, and where there is renunciation peace will follow.

मय्येव मन आधत्स्व मयि बुद्धिं निवेशय ।
निवसिष्यसि मय्येव अत ऊर्ध्वं न संशयः ॥ ८
अथ चित्तं समाधातुं न शक्नोषि मयि स्थिरम् ।
अभ्यासयोगेन ततो मामिच्छाप्तुं धनंजय ॥ ९
अभ्यासेऽप्यसमर्थोऽसि मत्कर्मपरमो भव ।
मदर्थमपि कर्माणि कुर्वन्सिद्धिमवाप्स्यसि ॥ १०
अथैतदप्यशक्तोऽसि कर्तुं मद्योगमाश्रितः ।
सर्वकर्मफलत्यागं ततः कुरु यतात्मवान् ॥ ११
श्रेयो हि ज्ञानमभ्यासाज्ज्ञानाद्ध्यानं विशिष्यते ।
ध्यानात्कर्मफलत्यागस्त्यागाच्छान्तिरनन्तरम् ॥ १२

He who is incapable of hatred towards any being, who is kind and compassionate, free from selfishness, without pride, equable in pleasure and in pain, and forgiving,

Always contented, self-centred, self-controlled, resolute, with mind and reason dedicated to Me, such a devotee of Mine is My beloved.

He who does not harm the world, and whom the world cannot harm, who is not carried away by any impulse of joy, anger or fear, such a one is My beloved.

He who expects nothing, who is pure, watchful, indifferent, unruffled, and who renounces all initiative, such a one is My beloved.

He who is beyond joy and hate, who neither laments nor desires, to whom good and evil fortunes are the same, such a one is My beloved.

He to whom friend and foe are alike, who welcomes equally honour and dishonour, heat and cold, pleasure and pain, who is enamoured of nothing,

Who is indifferent to praise and censure, who enjoys silence, who is contented with every fate, who has no fixed abode, who is steadfast in mind, and filled with devotion, such a one is My beloved.

Verily those who love the spiritual wisdom as I have taught, whose faith never fails, and who concentrate their whole nature on Me, they indeed are My most beloved."

Thus, in the Holy Book the Bhagavad Gita, one of the Upanishads, in the Science of the Supreme Spirit, in the Art of Self-Knowledge, in the colloquy between the Divine Lord Shri Krishna and the Prince Arjuna, stands the twelfth chapter, entitled: Bhakti-Yoga or the Path of Love.

अद्वेष्टा सर्वभूतानां मैत्रः करुण एव च ।
निर्ममो निरहंकारः समदुःखसुखः क्षमी ॥ १३
संतुष्टः सततं योगी यतात्मा दृढनिश्चयः ।
मय्यर्पितमनोबुद्धियों मद्भक्तः स मे प्रियः ॥ १४
यस्मान्नोद्विजते लोको लोकान्नोद्विजते च यः ।
हर्षामर्षभयोद्वेगैर्मुक्तो यः स च मे प्रियः ॥ १५
अनपेक्षः शुचिर्दक्ष उदासीनो गतव्यथः ।
सर्वारम्भपरित्यागी यो मद्भक्तः स मे प्रियः ॥ १६
यो न हृष्यति न द्वेष्टि न शोचति न काङ्क्षति ।
शुभाशुभपरित्यागी भक्तिमान्यः स मे प्रियः ॥ १७
समः शत्रौ च मित्रे च तथा मानावमानयोः ।
शीतोष्णसुखदुःखेषु समः सङ्गविवर्जितः ॥ १८
तुल्यनिन्दास्तुतिर्मौनी संतुष्टो येन केनचित् ।
अनिकेतः स्थिरमतिर्भक्तिमान्मे प्रियो नरः ॥ १९
ये तु धर्म्यामृतमिदं यथोक्तं पर्युपासते ।
श्रद्दधाना मत्परमा भक्तास्तेऽतीव मे प्रियाः ॥ २०

इति श्रीमद्भगवद्गीतासु द्वादशोऽध्यायः ॥ १२ ॥

THIRTEEN

·१३·

SPIRIT AND MATTER

अर्जुन उवाच ।
प्रकृतिं पुरुषं चैव क्षेत्रं क्षेत्रज्ञमेव च ।
एतद्वेदितुमिच्छामि ज्ञानं ज्ञेयं च केशव ॥

श्रीभगवानुवाच ।
इदं शरीरं कौन्तेय क्षेत्रमित्यभिधीयते ।
एतद्यो वेत्ति तं प्राहुः क्षेत्रज्ञ इति तद्विदः ॥ १

क्षेत्रज्ञं चापि मां विद्धि सर्वक्षेत्रेषु भारत ।
क्षेत्रक्षेत्रज्ञयोर्ज्ञानं यत्तज्ज्ञानं मतं मम ॥ २

तत्क्षेत्रं यच्च यादृक्च यद्विकारि यतश्च यत् ।
स च यो यत्प्रभावश्च तत्समासेन मे शृणु ॥ ३

ऋषिभिर्बहुधा गीतं छन्दोभिर्विविधैः पृथक् ।
ब्रह्मसूत्रपदैश्चैव हेतुमद्भिर्विनिश्चितैः ॥ ४

महाभूतान्यहंकारो बुद्धिरव्यक्तमेव च ।
इन्द्रियाणि दशैकं च पञ्च चेन्द्रियगोचराः ॥ ५

इच्छा द्वेषः सुखं दुःखं संघातश्चेतना धृतिः ।
एतत्क्षेत्रं समासेन सविकारमुदाहृतम् ॥ ६

अमानित्वमदम्भित्वमहिंसा क्षान्तिरार्जवम् ।
आचार्योपासनं शौचं स्थैर्यमात्मविनिग्रहः ॥ ७

इन्द्रियार्थेषु वैराग्यमनहंकार एव च ।
जन्ममृत्युजराव्याधिदुःखदोषानुदर्शनम् ॥ ८
असक्तिरनभिष्वङ्गः पुत्रदारगृहादिषु ।
नित्यं च समचित्तत्वमिष्टानिष्टोपपत्तिषु ॥ ९
मयि चान्यन्ययोगेन भक्तिरव्यभिचारिणी ।
विविक्तदेशसेवित्वमरतिर्जनसंसदि ॥ १०
अध्यात्मज्ञाननित्यत्वं तत्त्वज्ञानार्थदर्शनम् ।
एतज्ज्ञानमिति प्रोक्तमज्ञानं यदतोऽन्यथा ॥ ११

"*Arjuna asked:* My Lord! Who is God and what is Nature; what is Matter and what is the Self; what is that they call Wisdom, and what is it that is worth knowing? I wish to have this explained.

Lord Shri Krishna replied: O Arjuna! The body of man is the playground of the Self; and That which knows the activities of Matter, sages call the Self.

I am the Omniscient Self that abides in the playground of Matter; knowledge of Matter and of the all-knowing Self is wisdom.

What is called Matter, of what it is composed, whence it came, and why it changes, what the Self is, and what Its power—this I will now briefly set forth.

Seers have sung of It in various ways, in many hymns and sacred Vedic songs, weighty in thought and convincing in argument.

The five great fundamentals (earth, fire, air, water and ether), personality, intellect, the mysterious life force, the ten organs of perception and action, the mind and the five domains of sensation;

Desire, aversion, pleasure, pain, sympathy, vitality and the persistent clinging to life, these are in brief the constituents of changing Matter.

Humility, sincerity, harmlessness, forgiveness, rectitude, service of the Master, purity, steadfastness, self-control;

Renunciation of the delights of sense, absence of pride, right understanding of the painful problems of birth and death, of age and sickness;

Indifference, non-attachment to sex, progeny or home, equanimity in good fortune and in bad;

Unswerving devotion to Me, by concentration on Me and Me alone, a love for solitude, indifference to social life;

Constant yearning for the knowledge of Self, and pondering over the lessons of the great Truth—this is Wisdom, all else ignorance.

ज्ञेयं यत्तत्प्रवक्ष्यामि यज्ज्ञात्वामृतमश्नुते ।
अनादिमत्परं ब्रह्म न सत्तन्नासदुच्यते ॥ १२
सर्वतःपाणिपादं तत्सर्वतोक्षिशिरोमुखम् ।
सर्वतःश्रुतिमल्लोके सर्वमावृत्य तिष्ठति ॥ १३
सर्वेन्द्रियगुणाभासं सर्वेन्द्रियविवर्जितम् ।
असक्तं सर्वभृच्चैव निर्गुणं गुणभोक्तृ च ॥ १४
बहिरन्तश्च भूतानामचरं चरमेव च ।
सूक्ष्मत्वात्तदविज्ञेयं दूरस्थं चान्तिके च तत् ॥ १५
अविभक्तं च भूतेषु विभक्तमिव च स्थितम् ।
भूतभर्तृ च तज्ज्ञेयं ग्रसिष्णु प्रभविष्णु च ॥ १६
ज्योतिषामपि तज्ज्योतिस्तमसः परमुच्यते ।
ज्ञानं ज्ञेयं ज्ञानगम्यं हृदि सर्वस्य विष्ठितम् ॥ १७
इति क्षेत्रं तथा ज्ञानं ज्ञेयं चोक्तं समासतः ।
मद्भक्त एतद्विज्ञाय मद्भावायोपपद्यते ॥ १८

I will speak to thee now of that great Truth which man ought to know, since by its means he will win immortal bliss — that which is without beginning, the Eternal Spirit which dwells in Me, neither with form, nor yet without it.

Everywhere are Its hands and Its feet, everywhere It has eyes that see, heads that think and mouths that speak; everywhere It listens; It dwells in all the worlds; It envelops them all.

Beyond the senses, It yet shines through every sense perception. Bound to nothing, It yet sustains everything. Unaffected by the Qualities, It still enjoys them all.

It is within all beings, yet outside; motionless yet moving; too subtle to be perceived; far away yet always near.

In all beings undivided, yet living in division, It is the upholder of all, Creator and Destroyer alike;

It is the Light of lights, beyond the reach of darkness; the Wisdom, the only thing that is worth knowing or that wisdom can teach; the Presence in the hearts of all.

Thus have I told thee in brief what Matter is, and the Self worth realising and what is Wisdom. He who is devoted to Me knows; and assuredly he will enter into Me.

प्रकृतिं पुरुषं चैव विद्ध्यनादी उभावपि ।
विकारांश्च गुणांश्चैव विद्धि प्रकृतिसंभवान् ॥ १९

कार्यकारणकर्तृत्वे हेतुः प्रकृतिरुच्यते ।
पुरुषः सुखदुःखानां भोक्तृत्वे हेतुरुच्यते ॥ २०

पुरुषः प्रकृतिस्थो हि भुङ्क्ते प्रकृतिजान्गुणान् ।
कारणं गुणसङ्गोऽस्य सदसद्योनिजन्मसु ॥ २१

उपद्रष्टानुमन्ता च भर्ता भोक्ता महेश्वरः ।
परमात्मेति चाप्युक्तो देहेऽस्मिन्पुरुषः परः ॥ २२

य एवं वेत्ति पुरुषं प्रकृतिं च गुणैः सह ।
सर्वथा वर्तमानोऽपि न स भूयोऽभिजायते ॥ २३

Know thou further that Nature and God have no beginning; and that differences of character and quality have their origin in Nature only.

Nature is the Law which generates cause and effect; God is the source of the enjoyment of all pleasure and pain.

God dwelling in the heart of Nature experiences the Qualities which Nature brings forth; and His affinity towards the Qualities is the reason for His living in a good or evil body.

Thus in the body of man dwells the Supreme God; He who sees and permits, upholds and enjoys, the Highest God and the Highest Self.

He who understands God and Nature along with her Qualities, whatever be his condition in life, he comes not again to earth.

ध्यानेनात्मनि पश्यन्ति केचिदात्मानमात्मना ।
अन्ये सांख्येन योगेन कर्मयोगेन चापरे ॥ २४

अन्ये त्वेवमजानन्तः श्रुत्वान्येभ्य उपासते ।
तेऽपि चातितरन्त्येव मृत्युं श्रुतिपरायणाः ॥ २५

यावत्संजायते किंचित्सत्त्वं स्थावरजङ्गमम् ।
क्षेत्रक्षेत्रज्ञसंयोगात्तद्विद्धि भरतर्षभ ॥ २६

समं सर्वेषु भूतेषु तिष्ठन्तं परमेश्वरम् ।
विनश्यत्स्वविनश्यन्तं यः पश्यति स पश्यति ॥ २७

समं पश्यन्हि सर्वत्र समवस्थितमीश्वरम् ।
न हिनस्त्यात्मनात्मानं ततो याति परां गतिम् ॥ २८

प्रकृत्यैव च कर्माणि क्रियमाणानि सर्वशः ।
यः पश्यति तथात्मानमकर्तारं स पश्यति ॥ २९

यदा भूतपृथग्भावमेकस्थमनुपश्यति ।
तत एव च विस्तारं ब्रह्म संपद्यते तदा ॥ ३०

अनादित्वान्निर्गुणत्वात्परमात्मायमव्ययः ।
शरीरस्थोऽपि कौन्तेय न करोति न लिप्यते ॥ ३१

यथा सर्वगतं सौक्ष्म्यादाकाशं नोपलिप्यते ।
सर्वत्रावस्थितो देहे तथात्मा नोपलिप्यते ॥ ३२

यथा प्रकाशयत्येकः कृत्स्नं लोकमिमं रविः ।
क्षेत्रं क्षेत्री तथा कृत्स्नं प्रकाशयति भारत ॥ ३३

क्षेत्रक्षेत्रज्ञयोरेवमन्तरं ज्ञानचक्षुषा ।
भूतप्रकृतिमोक्षं च ये विदुर्यान्ति ते परम् ॥ ३४

इति श्रीमद्भगवद्गीतासु त्रयोदशोऽध्यायः ॥ १३ ॥

Some realise the Supreme by meditating, by Its aid, on the Self within, others by pure reason, others by right action.

Others again, having no direct knowledge but only hearing from others, nevertheless worship, and they, too, if true to the teachings, cross the sea of death.

Wherever life is seen in things movable or immovable, it is the joint product of Matter and Spirit.

He who can see the Supreme Lord in all beings, the Imperishable amidst the perishable, he it is who really sees.

Beholding the Lord in all things equally, his actions do not mar his spiritual life but lead him to the height of Bliss.

He who understands that it is only the Law of Nature that brings action to fruition, and that the Self never acts, alone knows the Truth.

He who sees the diverse forms of life all rooted in the One, and growing forth from Him, he shall indeed find the Absolute.

The Supreme Spirit, O Prince, is without beginning, without Qualities and Imperishable, and though it be within the body, yet It does not act, nor is It affected by action.

As space, though present everywhere, remains by reason of its subtlety unaffected, so the Self, though present in all forms, retains its purity unalloyed.

As the one Sun illuminates the whole earth, so the Lord illumines the whole universe.

Those who with the eyes of wisdom thus see the difference between Matter and Spirit, and know how to liberate Life from the Law of Nature, they attain the Supreme."

Thus, in the Holy Book the Bhagavad Gita, one of the Upanishads, in the Science of the Supreme Spirit, in the Art of Self-Knowledge, in the colloquy between the Divine Lord Shri Krishna and the Prince Arjuna, stands the thirteenth chapter, entitled: Spirit and Matter.

FOURTEEN
·१४·
THE THREE QUALITIES

"*Lord Shri Krishna continued:* Now I will reveal unto thee the Wisdom which is beyond knowledge, by attaining which the sages have reached Perfection.

Dwelling in Wisdom and realising My Divinity, they are not born again when the universe is re-created at the beginning of every cycle, nor are they affected when it is dissolved.

The eternal Cosmos is My womb, in which I plant the seed, from which all beings are born, O Prince!

O illustrious son of Kunti! Through whatever wombs men are born, it is the Spirit Itself that conceives, and I am their Father.

Purity, Passion and Ignorance are the Qualities which the Law of Nature bringeth forth. They fetter the free Spirit in all beings.

O Sinless One! Of these, Purity, being luminous, strong and invulnerable, binds one by its yearning for happiness and illumination.

Passion, engendered by thirst for pleasure and attachment, binds the soul through its fondness for activity.

But Ignorance, the product of darkness, stupefies the senses in all embodied beings, binding them by the chains of folly, indolence and lethargy.

Purity brings happiness, Passion commotion, and Ignorance, which obscures wisdom, leads to a life of failure.

श्रीभगवानुवाच ।
परं भूयः प्रवक्ष्यामि ज्ञानानां ज्ञानमुत्तमम् ।
यज्ज्ञात्वा मुनयः सर्वे परां सिद्धिमितो गताः ॥ १
इदं ज्ञानमुपाश्रित्य मम साधर्म्यमागताः ।
सर्गेऽपि नोपजायन्ते प्रलये न व्यथन्ति च ॥ २
मम योनिर्महद्ब्रह्म तस्मिन्गर्भं दधाम्यहम् ।
संभवः सर्वभूतानां ततो भवति भारत ॥ ३
सर्वयोनिषु कौन्तेय मूर्तयः संभवन्ति याः ।
तासां ब्रह्म महद्योनिरहं बीजप्रदः पिता ॥ ४
सत्त्वं रजस्तम इति गुणाः प्रकृतिसंभवाः ।
निबध्नन्ति महाबाहो देहे देहिनमव्ययम् ॥ ५
तत्र सत्त्वं निर्मलत्वात्प्रकाशकमनामयम् ।
सुखसङ्गेन बध्नाति ज्ञानसङ्गेन चानघ ॥ ६
रजो रागात्मकं विद्धि तृष्णासङ्गसमुद्भवम् ।
तन्निबध्नाति कौन्तेय कर्मसङ्गेन देहिनम् ॥ ७
तमस्त्वज्ञानजं विद्धि मोहनं सर्वदेहिनाम् ।
प्रमादालस्यनिद्राभिस्तन्निबध्नाति भारत ॥ ८
सत्त्वं सुखे सञ्जयति रजः कर्मणि भारत ।
ज्ञानमावृत्य तु तमः प्रमादे सञ्जयत्युत ॥ ९

134

O Prince! Purity prevails when Passion and Ignorance are overcome; Passion, when Purity and Ignorance are overcome; and Ignorance when it overcomes Purity and Passion.

When the light of knowledge gleams forth from all the gates of the body, then be sure that Purity prevails.

O best of Indians! Avarice, the impulse to act and the beginning of action itself are all due to the dominance of Passion.

Darkness, stagnation, folly and infatuation are the result of the domination of Ignorance, O joy of the Kuru-clan!

When Purity prevails, the soul on quitting the body passes on to the pure regions where live those who know the Highest.

When Passion prevails, the soul is reborn among those who love activity; when Ignorance rules, it enters the wombs of the ignorant.

They say the fruit of a meritorious action is spotless and full of Purity; the outcome of Passion is misery, and of Ignorance darkness.

Purity engenders Wisdom, Passion avarice, and Ignorance folly, infatuation and darkness.

When Purity is in the ascendant, the man evolves; when Passion, he neither evolves nor degenerates; when Ignorance, he is lost.

As soon as a man understands that it is only the Qualities which act and nothing else, and perceives That which is beyond, he attains My divine nature.

When the soul transcends the Qualities, which are the real cause of physical existence, then, freed from birth and death, from old age and misery, he quaffs the nectar of immortality.

रजस्तमश्चाभिभूय सत्त्वं भवति भारत ।
रजः सत्त्वं तमश्चैव तमः सत्त्वं रजस्तथा ॥ १०
सर्वद्वारेषु देहेऽस्मिन्प्रकाश उपजायते ।
ज्ञानं यदा तदा विद्याद्विवृद्धं सत्त्वमित्युत ॥ ११
लोभः प्रवृत्तिरारम्भः कर्मणामशमः स्पृहा ।
रजस्येतानि जायन्ते विवृद्धे भरतर्षभ ॥ १२
अप्रकाशोऽप्रवृत्तिश्च प्रमादो मोह एव च ।
तमस्येतानि जायन्ते विवृद्धे कुरुनन्दन ॥ १३
यदा सत्त्वे प्रवृद्धे तु प्रलयं याति देहभृत् ।
तदोत्तमविदां लोकानमलान्प्रतिपद्यते ॥ १४
रजसि प्रलयं गत्वा कर्मसङ्गिषु जायते ।
तथा प्रलीनस्तमसि मूढयोनिषु जायते ॥ १५
कर्मणः सुकृतस्याहुः सात्त्विकं निर्मलं फलम् ।
रजसस्तु फलं दुःखमज्ञानं तमसः फलम् ॥ १६
सत्त्वात्संजायते ज्ञानं रजसो लोभ एव च ।
प्रमादमोहौ तमसो भवतोऽज्ञानमेव च ॥ १७
ऊर्ध्वं गच्छन्ति सत्त्वस्था मध्ये तिष्ठन्ति राजसाः ।
जघन्यगुणवृत्तस्था अधो गच्छन्ति तामसाः ॥ १८
नान्यं गुणेभ्यः कर्तारं यदा द्रष्टानुपश्यति ।
गुणेभ्यश्च परं वेत्ति मद्भावं सोऽधिगच्छति ॥ १९
गुणानेतानतीत्य त्रीन्देही देहसमुद्भवान् ।
जन्ममृत्युजरादुःखैर्विमुक्तोऽमृतमश्नुते ॥ २०

अर्जुन उवाच ।
कैर्लिङ्गैस्त्रीन्गुणानेतानतीतो भवति प्रभो ।
किमाचारः कथं चैतांस्त्रीन्गुणानतिवर्तते ॥ २१

श्रीभगवानुवाच ।
प्रकाशं च प्रवृत्तिं च मोहमेव च पाण्डव ।
न द्वेष्टि संप्रवृत्तानि न निवृत्तानि काङ्क्षति ॥ २२
उदासीनवदासीनो गुणैर्यो न विचाल्यते ।
गुणा वर्तन्त इत्येव योऽवतिष्ठति नेङ्गते ॥ २३
समदुःखसुखः स्वस्थः समलोष्टाश्मकाञ्चनः ।
तुल्यप्रियाप्रियो धीरस्तुल्यनिन्दात्मसंस्तुतिः ॥ २४
मानावमानयोस्तुल्यस्तुल्यो मित्रारिपक्षयोः ।
सर्वारम्भपरित्यागी गुणातीतः स उच्यते ॥ २५
मां च योऽव्यभिचारेण भक्तियोगेन सेवते ।
स गुणान्समतीत्यैतान्ब्रह्मभूयाय कल्पते ॥ २६
ब्रह्मणो हि प्रतिष्ठाहममृतस्याव्ययस्य च ।
शाश्वतस्य च धर्मस्य सुखस्यैकान्तिकस्य च ॥ २७

इति श्रीमद्भगवद्गीतासु चतुर्दशोऽध्यायः ॥ १४ ॥

Arjuna asked: My Lord! By what signs can he who has transcended the Qualities be recognised? How does he act? How does he live beyond them?

Lord Shri Krishna replied: O Prince! He who shuns not the Quality which is present, and longs not for that which is absent;

He who maintains an attitude of indifference, who is not disturbed by the Qualities, who realises that it is only they who act, and remains calm;

Who accepts pleasure or pain as it comes, is centred in his Self, to whom a piece of clay or a stone or gold are the same, who neither likes nor dislikes, who is steadfast, indifferent alike to praise or censure;

Who looks equally upon honour and dishonour, loves friends and foes alike, abandons all initiative, such is he who transcends the Qualities.

And he who serves Me and only Me, with unfaltering devotion, shall overcome the Qualities, and become One with the Eternal.

For I am the Home of the Spirit, the continual Source of immortality, of eternal Righteousness and of infinite Joy."

Thus, in the Holy Book the Bhagavad Gita, one of the Upanishads, in the Science of the Supreme Spirit, in the Art of Self-Knowledge, in the colloquy between the Divine Lord Shri Krishna and the Prince Arjuna, stands the fourteenth chapter, entitled: The Three Qualities.

FIFTEEN

·§4·

THE LORD-GOD

श्रीभगवानुवाच ।
ऊर्ध्वमूलमधःशाखमश्वत्थं प्राहुरव्ययम् ।
छन्दांसि यस्य पर्णानि यस्तं वेद स वेदवित् ॥ १
अधश्चोर्ध्वं प्रसृतास्तस्य शाखा
गुणप्रवृद्धा विषयप्रवालाः ।
अधश्च मूलान्यनुसंततानि
कर्मानुबन्धीनि मनुष्यलोके ॥ २
न रूपमस्येह तथोपलभ्यते
नान्तो न चादिर्न च संप्रतिष्ठा ।
अश्वत्थमेनं सुविरूढमूल-
मसङ्गशस्त्रेण दृढेन छित्त्वा ॥ ३

ततः पदं तत्परिमार्गितव्यं
यस्मिन्गता न निवर्तन्ति भूयः ।
तमेव चाद्यं पुरुषं प्रपद्ये
यतः प्रवृत्तिः प्रसृता पुराणी ॥ ४
निर्मानमोहा जितसङ्गदोषा
अध्यात्मनित्या विनिवृत्तकामाः ।
द्वन्द्वैर्विमुक्ताः सुखदुःखसंज्ञै-
र्गच्छन्त्यमूढाः पदमव्ययं तत् ॥ ५
न तद्भासयते सूर्यो न शशाङ्को न पावकः ।
यद्गत्वा न निवर्तन्ते तद्धाम परमं मम ॥ ६
ममैवांशो जीवलोके जीवभूतः सनातनः ।
मनःषष्ठानीन्द्रियाणि प्रकृतिस्थानि कर्षति ॥ ७
शरीरं यदवाप्नोति यच्चाप्युत्क्रामतीश्वरः ।
गृहीत्वैतानि संयाति वायुर्गन्धानिवाशयात् ॥ ८

श्रोत्रं चक्षुः स्पर्शनं च रसनं घ्राणमेव च ।
अधिष्ठाय मनश्चायं विषयानुपसेवते ॥ ९
उत्क्रामन्तं स्थितं वापि भुञ्जानं वा गुणान्वितम् ।
विमूढा नानुपश्यन्ति पश्यन्ति ज्ञानचक्षुषः ॥ १०
यतन्तो योगिनश्चैनं पश्यन्त्यात्मन्यवस्थितम् ।
यतन्तोऽप्यकृतात्मानो नैनं पश्यन्त्यचेतसः ॥ ११

140

"*Lord Shri Krishna continued:* This phenomenal creation, which is both ephemeral and eternal, is like a tree, but having its seed above in the Highest and its ramifications on this earth below. The scriptures are its leaves, and he who understands this, knows.

Its branches shoot upwards and downwards, deriving their nourishment from the Qualities; its buds are the objects of sense; and its roots, which follow the Law causing man's regeneration and degeneration, pierce downwards into the soil.

In this world its true form is not known, neither its origin nor its end, and its strength is not understood, until the tree with its roots striking deep into the earth is hewn down by the sharp axe of non-attachment.

Beyond lies the Path, from which, when found, there is no return. This is the Primal God from whence this ancient creation has sprung.

The wise attain Eternity when, freed from pride and delusion, they have conquered their love for the things of sense; when, renouncing desire and fixing their gaze on the Self, they have ceased to be tossed to and fro by the opposing sensations, like pleasure and pain.

Neither sun, moon, nor fire shines there. Those who go thither never come back. For, O Arjuna, that is My Celestial Home!

It is only a very small part of My Eternal Self, which is the life of this universe, drawing round itself the six senses, the mind the last, which have their source in Nature.

When the Supreme Lord enters a body or leaves it, He gathers these senses together and travels on with them, as the wind gathers perfume while passing through the flowers.

He is the perception of the ear, the eye, the touch, the taste and the smell, yea and of the mind also; and the enjoyment of the things which they perceive is also His.

The ignorant do not see that it is He Who is present in life and Who departs at death or even that it is He Who enjoys pleasure through the Qualities. Only the eye of wisdom sees.

The saints with great effort find Him within themselves; but not the unintelligent, who in spite of every effort cannot control their minds.

यदादित्यगतं तेजो जगद्भासयतेऽखिलम् ।
यच्चन्द्रमसि यच्चाग्नौ तत्तेजो विद्धि मामकम् ॥ १२

गामाविश्य च भूतानि धारयाम्यहमोजसा ।
पुष्णामि चौषधीः सर्वाः सोमो भूत्वा रसात्मकः ॥ १३

अहं वैश्वानरो भूत्वा प्राणिनां देहमाश्रितः ।
प्राणापानसमायुक्तः पचाम्यन्नं चतुर्विधम् ॥ १४

सर्वस्य चाहं हृदि सन्निविष्टो
    मत्तः स्मृतिर्ज्ञानमपोहनं च ।
वेदैश्च सर्वैरहमेव वेद्यो
    वेदान्तकृद्वेदविदेव चाहम् ॥ १५

द्वाविमौ पुरुषौ लोके क्षरश्चाक्षर एव च ।
क्षरः सर्वाणि भूतानि कूटस्थोऽक्षर उच्यते ॥ १६

उत्तमः पुरुषस्त्वन्यः परमात्मेत्युदाहृतः ।
यो लोकत्रयमाविश्य बिभर्त्यव्यय ईश्वरः ॥ १७

यस्मात्क्षरमतीतोऽहमक्षरादपि चोत्तमः ।
अतोऽस्मि लोके वेदे च प्रथितः पुरुषोत्तमः ॥ १८

यो मामेवमसंमूढो जानाति पुरुषोत्तमम् ।
स सर्वविद्भजति मां सर्वभावेन भारत ॥ १९

इति गुह्यतमं शास्त्रमिदमुक्तं मयानघ ।
एतद्बुद्ध्वा बुद्धिमान्स्यात्कृतकृत्यश्च भारत ॥ २०

इति श्रीमद्भगवद्गीतासु पञ्चदशोऽध्यायः ॥ १५ ॥

Remember that the Light which, proceeding from the sun, illumines the whole world, and the Light which is in the moon, and That which is in the fire also, all are born of Me.

I enter this world and animate all My creatures with My vitality; and by My cool moonbeams I nourish the plants.

Becoming the fire of life, I pass into their bodies and, uniting with the vital streams of Prana and Apana, I digest the various kinds of food.

I am enthroned in the hearts of all; memory, wisdom and discrimination owe their origin to Me. I am He Who is to be realised in the scriptures; I inspire their wisdom and I know their truth.

There are two aspects in Nature: the perishable and the imperishable. All life in this world belongs to the former, the unchanging element belongs to the latter.

But higher than all am I, the Supreme God, the Absolute Self, the Eternal Lord, Who pervades the worlds and upholds them all.

Beyond comparison of the Eternal with the non-eternal am I, Who am called by scriptures and sages the Supreme Personality, the Highest God.

He who with unclouded vision sees Me as the Lord-God, knows all there is to be known, and always shall worship Me with his whole heart.

Thus, O Sinless One, I have revealed to thee this most mystic knowledge. He who understands gains wisdom and attains the consummation of life."

Thus, in the Holy Book the Bhagavad Gita, one of the Upanishads, in the Science of the Supreme Spirit, in the Art of Self-Knowledge, in the colloquy between the Divine Lord Shri Krishna and the Prince Arjuna, stands the fifteenth chapter, entitled: The Lord-God.

SIXTEEN
·१६·
DIVINE AND DEMONIC
CIVILISATION

श्रीभगवानुवाच ।

अभयं सत्त्वसंशुद्धिर्ज्ञानयोगव्यवस्थितिः ।
दानं दमश्च यज्ञश्च स्वाध्यायस्तप आर्जवम् ॥ १

अहिंसा सत्यमक्रोधस्त्यागः शान्तिरपैशुनम् ।
दया भूतेष्वलोलुप्त्वं मार्दवं ह्रीरचापलम् ॥ २

तेजः क्षमा धृतिः शौचमद्रोहो नातिमानिता ।
भवन्ति संपदं दैवीमभिजातस्य भारत ॥ ३

दम्भो दर्पोऽतिमानश्च क्रोधः पारुष्यमेव च ।
अज्ञानं चाभिजातस्य पार्थ संपदमासुरीम् ॥ ४

दैवी संपद्विमोक्षाय निबन्धायासुरी मता ।
मा शुचः संपदं दैवीमभिजातोऽसि पाण्डव ॥ ५

द्वौ भूतसर्गौ लोकेऽस्मिन्दैव आसुर एव च ।
दैवो विस्तरशः प्रोक्त आसुरं पार्थ मे शृणु ॥ ६

प्रवृत्तिं च निवृत्तिं च जना न विदुरासुराः ।
न शौचं नापि चाचारो न सत्यं तेषु विद्यते ॥ ७

असत्यमप्रतिष्ठं ते जगदाहुरनीश्वरम् ।
अपरस्परसंभूतं किमन्यत्कामहैतुकम् ॥ ८

एतां दृष्टिमवष्टभ्य नष्टात्मानोऽल्पबुद्धयः ।
प्रभवन्त्युग्रकर्माणः क्षयाय जगतोऽहिताः ॥ ९

"Lord Shri Krishna continued: Fearlessness, clean living, unceasing concentration on wisdom, readiness to give, self-control, a spirit of sacrifice, regular study of the scriptures, austerities, candour,

Harmlessness, truth, absence of wrath, renunciation, contentment, straightforwardness, compassion towards all, uncovetousness, courtesy, modesty, constancy,

Valour, forgiveness, fortitude, purity, freedom from hate and vanity; these are his who possesses the Godly Qualities, O Arjuna!

Hypocrisy, pride, insolence, cruelty, ignorance belong to him who is born of the godless qualities.

Godly qualities lead to liberation; godless to bondage. Do not be anxious, Prince! Thou hast the Godly qualities.

All beings are of two classes: Godly and godless. The Godly I have described; I will now describe the other.

The godless do not know how to act or how to renounce. They have neither purity nor truth. They do not understand the right principles of conduct.

They say that the universe is an accident with no purpose and no God. Life is created by sexual union, a product of lust and nothing else.

Thinking thus, these degraded souls, these enemies of mankind—whose intelligence is negligible and whose deeds are monstrous—come into the world only to destroy.

कामाश्रित्य दुष्पूरं दम्भमानमदान्विताः ।
मोहाद्गृहीत्वासद्ग्राहान्प्रवर्तन्तेऽशुचिव्रताः ॥ १०
चिन्तापरिमेयां च प्रलयान्तामुपाश्रिताः ।
कामोपभोगपरमा एतावदिति निश्चिताः ॥ ११
आशापाशशतैर्बद्धाः कामक्रोधपरायणाः ।
ईहन्ते कामभोगार्थमन्यायेनार्थसंचयान् ॥ १२
इदमद्य मया लब्धमिदं प्राप्स्ये मनोरथम् ।
इदमस्तीदमपि मे भविष्यति पुनर्धनम् ॥ १३
असौ मया हतः शत्रुर्हनिष्ये चापरानपि ।
ईश्वरोऽहमहं भोगी सिद्धोऽहं बलवान्सुखी ॥ १४
आढ्योऽभिजनवानस्मि कोऽन्योऽस्ति सदृशो मया ।
यक्ष्ये दास्यामि मोदिष्य इत्यज्ञानविमोहिताः ॥ १५
अनेकचित्तविभ्रान्ता मोहजालसमावृताः ।
प्रसक्ताः कामभोगेषु पतन्ति नरकेऽशुचौ ॥ १६
आत्मसंभाविताः स्तब्धा धनमानमदान्विताः ।
यजन्ते नामयज्ञैस्ते दम्भेनाविधिपूर्वकम् ॥ १७
अहंकारं बलं दर्पं कामं क्रोधं च संश्रिताः ।
मामात्मपरदेहेषु प्रद्विषन्तोऽभ्यसूयकाः ॥ १८
तानहं द्विषतः क्रूरान्संसारेषु नराधमान् ।
क्षिपाम्यजस्रमशुभानासुरीष्वेव योनिषु ॥ १९
आसुरीं योनिमापन्ना मूढा जन्मनि जन्मनि ।
मामप्राप्यैव कौन्तेय ततो यान्त्यधमां गतिम् ॥ २०

Giving themselves up to insatiable passions, hypocritical, self-sufficient and arrogant, cherishing false conceptions founded on delusion, they work only to carry out their own unholy purposes.

Poring anxiously over evil resolutions, which only end in death; seeking only the gratification of desire as the highest goal; seeing nothing beyond;

Caught in the toils of a hundred vain hopes, the slaves of passion and of wrath, they accumulate hoards of unjust wealth, only to pander to their sensual desire.

This have I gained today; tomorrow I will gratify another desire; this wealth is mine now, the rest shall be mine ere long;

I have slain one enemy, I will slay the others also; I am worthy to enjoy, I am the Almighty, I am perfect, powerful and happy;

I am rich, I am well-bred; who is there to compare with me? I will sacrifice, I will give, I will pay—and I will enjoy. Thus blinded by ignorance,

Perplexed by discordant thoughts, entangled in the snares of desire, infatuated by passion, they sink into the horrors of hell.

Self-conceited, stubborn, rich, proud and insolent, they make a display of their patronage, disregarding the rules of decency.

Puffed up by power and inordinate conceit, swayed by lust and wrath, these wicked people hate Me Who am within them, as I am within all.

Those who thus hate Me, who are cruel, the dregs of mankind, I condemn them to a continuous, miserable and godless rebirth.

So reborn, they spend life after life, enveloped in delusion. And they never reach Me, O Prince, but degenerate into still lower forms of life.

त्रिविधं नरकस्येदं द्वारं नाशनमात्मनः ।
कामः क्रोधस्तथा लोभस्तस्मादेतत्त्रयं त्यजेत् ॥ २१
एतैर्विमुक्तः कौन्तेय तमोद्वारैस्त्रिभिर्नरः ।
आचरत्यात्मनः श्रेयस्ततो याति परां गतिम् ॥ २२
यः शास्त्रविधिमुत्सृज्य वर्तते कामकारतः ।
न स सिद्धिमवाप्नोति न सुखं न परां गतिम् ॥ २३
तस्माच्छास्त्रं प्रमाणं ते कार्याकार्यव्यवस्थितौ ।
ज्ञात्वा शास्त्रविधानोक्तं कर्म कर्तुमिहार्हसि ॥ २४

इति श्रीमद्भगवद्गीतासु षोडशोऽध्यायः ॥ १६ ॥

The gates of hell are three: lust, wrath and avarice. They destroy the Self. Avoid them.

These are the gates which lead to darkness; if a man avoids them he will ensure his own welfare, and in the end will attain his liberation.

But he who neglects the commands of the scriptures, and follows the promptings of passion, he does not attain perfection, happiness or the final goal.

Therefore whenever there is a doubt whether thou shouldst do a thing or not, let the scriptures guide thy conduct. In the light of the scriptures shouldst thou labour the whole of thy life."

Thus, in the Holy Book the Bhagavad Gita, one of the Upanishads, in the Science of the Supreme Spirit, in the Art of Self-Knowledge, in the colloquy between the Divine Lord Shri Krishna and the Prince Arjuna, stands the sixteenth chapter, entitled: Divine and Demonic Civilisation.

SEVENTEEN

THE THREEFOLD FAITH

अर्जुन उवाच ।
ये शास्त्रविधिमुत्सृज्य यजन्ते श्रद्धयान्विताः ।
तेषां निष्ठा तु का कृष्ण सत्त्वमाहो रजस्तमः ॥ १

श्रीभगवानुवाच ।
त्रिविधा भवति श्रद्धा देहिनां सा स्वभावजा ।
सात्त्विकी राजसी चैव तामसी चेति तां शृणु ॥ २
सत्त्वानुरूपा सर्वस्य श्रद्धा भवति भारत ।
श्रद्धामयोऽयं पुरुषो यो यच्छ्रद्धः स एव सः ॥ ३
यजन्ते सात्त्विका देवान्यक्षरक्षांसि राजसाः ।
प्रेतान्भूतगणांश्चान्ये यजन्ते तामसा जनाः ॥ ४
अशास्त्रविहितं घोरं तप्यन्ते ये तपो जनाः ।
दम्भाहंकारसंयुक्ताः कामरागबलान्विताः ॥ ५
कर्षयन्तः शरीरस्थं भूतग्राममचेतसः ।
मां चैवान्तःशरीरस्थं तान्विद्ध्यासुरनिश्चयान् ॥ ६

"*Arjuna asked:* My Lord! Those who do acts of sacrifice, not according to the scriptures but nevertheless with implicit faith, what is their condition? Is it one of Purity, of Passion or of Ignorance?

Lord Shri Krishna replied: Man has an inherent faith in one or another of the Qualities—Purity, Passion and Ignorance. Now listen.

The faith of every man conforms to his nature. By nature he is full of faith. He is in fact what his faith makes him.

The Pure worship the true God; the Passionate, the powers of wealth and magic; the Ignorant, the spirits of the dead and of the lower orders of nature.

Those who practise austerities not commanded by scripture, who are slaves to hypocrisy and egotism, who are carried away by the fury of desire and passion,

They are ignorant. They torment the organs of the body; and they harass Me also, Who lives within. Know that they are devoted to evil.

आहारस्त्वपि सर्वस्य त्रिविधो भवति प्रियः ।
यज्ञस्तपस्तथा दानं तेषां भेदमिमं शृणु ॥ ७
आयुःसत्त्वबलारोग्यसुखप्रीतिविवर्धनाः ।
रस्याः स्निग्धाः स्थिरा हृद्या आहाराः सात्त्विकप्रियाः ८
कट्वम्ललवणात्युष्णतीक्ष्णरूक्षविदाहिनः ।
आहारा राजसस्येष्टा दुःखशोकामयप्रदाः ॥ ९
यातयामं गतरसं पूति पर्युषितं च यत् ।
उच्छिष्टमपि चामेध्यं भोजनं तामसप्रियम् ॥ १०
अफलाकाङ्क्षिभिर्यज्ञो विधिदृष्टो य इज्यते ।
यष्टव्यमेवेति मनः समाधाय स सात्त्विकः ॥ ११
अभिसंधाय तु फलं दम्भार्थमपि चैव यत् ।
इज्यते भरतश्रेष्ठ तं यज्ञं विद्धि राजसम् ॥ १२
विधिहीनमसृष्टान्नं मन्त्रहीनमदक्षिणम् ।
श्रद्धाविरहितं यज्ञं तामसं परिचक्षते ॥ १३

The food which men enjoy is also threefold, like the ways of sacrifice, austerity and almsgiving. Listen to the distinction.

The foods that prolong life and increase purity, vigour, health, cheerfulness and happiness are those that are delicious, soothing, substantial and agreeable. These are loved by the Pure.

Those in whom Passion is dominant like foods that are bitter, sour, salt, over-hot, pungent, dry and burning. These produce unhappiness, repentance and disease.

The Ignorant love food which is stale, not nourishing, putrid and corrupt, the leavings of others and unclean.

Sacrifice is Pure when it is offered by one who does not covet the fruit thereof, when it is done according to the commands of scripture, and with implicit faith that the sacrifice is a duty.

Sacrifice which is performed for the sake of its results, or for self-glorification—that, O best of Aryans, is the product of Passion.

Sacrifice that is contrary to scriptural command, that is unaccompanied by prayers or gifts of food or money, and is without faith—that is the product of Ignorance.

देवद्विजगुरुप्राज्ञपूजनं शौचमार्जवम् ।
ब्रह्मचर्यमहिंसा च शारीरं तप उच्यते ॥ १४
अनुद्वेगकरं वाक्यं सत्यं प्रियहितं च यत् ।
स्वाध्यायाभ्यसनं चैव वाङ्मयं तप उच्यते ॥ १५
मनःप्रसादः सौम्यत्वं मौनमात्मविनिग्रहः ।
भावसंशुद्धिरित्येतत्तपो मानसमुच्यते ॥ १६
श्रद्धया परया तप्तं तपस्तत्रिविधं नरैः ।
अफलाकाङ्क्षिभिर्युक्तैः सात्त्विकं परिचक्षते ॥ १७
सत्कारमानपूजार्थं तपो दम्भेन चैव यत् ।
क्रियते तदिह प्रोक्तं राजसं चलमध्रुवम् ॥ १८
मूढग्राहेणात्मनो यत्पीडया क्रियते तपः ।
परस्योत्सादनार्थं वा तत्तामसमुदाहृतम् ॥ १९

Worship of God and the Master; respect for the preacher and the philosopher; purity, rectitude, continence and harmlessness—all this is physical austerity.

Speech that hurts no one, that is true, is pleasant to listen to and beneficial, and the constant study of the scriptures—this is austerity in speech.

Serenity, kindness, silence, self-control and purity—this is austerity of mind.

These threefold austerities performed with faith, and without thought of reward, may truly be accounted Pure.

Austerity coupled with hypocrisy or performed for the sake of self-glorification, popularity or vanity, comes from Passion, and its result is always doubtful and temporary.

Austerity done under delusion, and accompanied with sorcery or torture to oneself or another, may be assumed to spring from Ignorance.

दातव्यमिति यद्दानं दीयतेऽनुपकारिणे ।
देशे काले च पात्रे च तद्दानं सात्त्विकं स्मृतम् ॥ २० ॥

यत्तु प्रत्युपकारार्थं फलमुद्दिश्य वा पुनः ।
दीयते च परिक्लिष्टं तद्दानं राजसं स्मृतम् ॥ २१ ॥

अदेशकाले यद्दानमपात्रेभ्यश्च दीयते ।
असत्कृतमवज्ञातं तत्तामसमुदाहृतम् ॥ २२ ॥

ॐ तत्सदिति निर्देशो ब्रह्मणस्त्रिविधः स्मृतः ।
ब्राह्मणास्तेन वेदाश्च यज्ञाश्च विहिताः पुरा ॥ २३ ॥

तस्मादोमित्युदाहृत्य यज्ञदानतपःक्रियाः ।
प्रवर्तन्ते विधानोक्ताः सततं ब्रह्मवादिनाम् ॥ २४ ॥

तदित्यनभिसंधाय फलं यज्ञतपःक्रियाः ।
दानक्रियाश्च विविधाः क्रियन्ते मोक्षकाङ्क्षिभिः ॥ २५ ॥

सद्भावे साधुभावे च सदित्येतत्प्रयुज्यते ।
प्रशस्ते कर्मणि तथा सच्छब्दः पार्थ युज्यते ॥ २६ ॥

यज्ञे तपसि दाने च स्थितिः सदिति चोच्यते ।
कर्म चैव तदर्थीयं सदित्येवाभिधीयते ॥ २७ ॥

अश्रद्धया हुतं दत्तं तपस्तप्तं कृतं च यत् ।
असदित्युच्यते पार्थ न च तत्प्रेत्य नो इह ॥ २८ ॥

इति श्रीमद्भगवद्गीतासु सप्तदशोऽध्यायः ॥ १७ ॥

The gift which is given without thought of recompense, in the belief that it ought to be made, in a fit place, at an opportune time and to a deserving person—such a gift is Pure.

That which is given for the sake of the results it will produce, or with the hope of recompense, or grudgingly—that may truly be said to be the outcome of Passion.

And that which is given at an unsuitable place or time or to one who is unworthy, or with disrespect or contempt—such a gift is the result of Ignorance.

'Om Tat Sat' is the triple designation of the Eternal Spirit, by which of old the Vedic scriptures, the ceremonials and the sacrifices were ordained.

Therefore all acts of sacrifice, gifts and austerities, prescribed by the scriptures, are always begun by those who understand the Spirit with the word Om.

Those who desire deliverance begin their acts of sacrifice, austerity or gift with the word 'Tat' (meaning 'That'), without thought of reward.

'Sat' means Reality or the highest Good, and also, O Arjuna, it is used to mean an action of exceptional merit.

Conviction in sacrifice, in austerity and in giving is also called 'Sat.' So too an action done only for the Lord's sake.

Whatsoever is done without faith, whether it be sacrifice, austerity or gift or anything else, is called 'Asat' (meaning 'Unreal') for it is the negation of 'Sat,' O Arjuna! Such an act has no significance, here or hereafter."

Thus, in the Holy Book the Bhagavad Gita, one of the Upanishads, in the Science of the Supreme Spirit, in the Art of Self-Knowledge, in the colloquy between the Divine Lord Shri Krishna and the Prince Arjuna, stands the seventeenth chapter, entitled: The Threefold Faith.

EIGHTEEN
·ۼ·
THE SPIRIT OF RENUNCIATION

"*Arjuna asked:* O Mighty One! I desire to know how relinquishing is distinguished from renunciation.

Lord Shri Krishna replied: The sages say that renunciation means forgoing an action which springs from desire; and relinquishing means the surrender of its fruit.

Some philosophers say that all action is evil and should be abandoned. Others that acts of sacrifice, benevolence and austerity should not be given up.

O best of Indians! Listen to my judgement as regards this problem. It has a threefold aspect.

Acts of sacrifice, benevolence and austerity should not be given up but should be performed, for they purify the aspiring soul.

But they should be done with detachment and without thought of recompense. This is my final judgement.

अर्जुन उवाच ।
संन्यासस्य महाबाहो तत्त्वमिच्छामि वेदितुम् ।
त्यागस्य च हृषीकेश पृथक्केशिनिषूदन ॥ १
श्रीभगवानुवाच ।
काम्यानां कर्मणां न्यासं संन्यासं कवयो विदुः ।
सर्वकर्मफलत्यागं प्राहुस्त्यागं विचक्षणाः ॥ २
त्याज्यं दोषवदित्येके कर्म प्राहुर्मनीषिणः ।
यज्ञदानतपःकर्म न त्याज्यमिति चापरे ॥ ३
निश्चयं श्रृणु मे तत्र त्यागे भरतसत्तम ।
त्यागो हि पुरुषव्याघ्र त्रिविधः संप्रकीर्तितः ॥ ४
यज्ञदानतपःकर्म न त्याज्यं कार्यमेव तत् ।
यज्ञो दानं तपश्चैव पावनानि मनीषिणाम् ॥ ५
एतान्यपि तु कर्माणि सङ्गं त्यक्त्वा फलानि च ।
कर्तव्यानीति मे पार्थ निश्चितं मतमुत्तमम् ॥ ६

नियतस्य तु संन्यासः कर्मणो नोपपद्यते ।
मोहात्तस्य परित्यागस्तामसः परिकीर्तितः ॥ ७

दुःखमित्येव यत्कर्म कायक्लेशभयात्यजेत् ।
स कृत्वा राजसं त्यागं नैव त्यागफलं लभेत् ॥ ८

कार्यमित्येव यत्कर्म नियतं क्रियतेऽर्जुन ।
सङ्गं त्यक्त्वा फलं चैव स त्यागः सात्त्विको मतः ॥ ९

न द्वेष्ट्यकुशलं कर्म कुशले नानुषज्जते ।
त्यागी सत्त्वसमाविष्टो मेधावी छिन्नसंशयः ॥ १०

न हि देहभृता शक्यं त्यक्तुं कर्माण्यशेषतः ।
यस्तु कर्मफलत्यागी स त्यागीत्यभिधीयते ॥ ११

अनिष्टमिष्टं मिश्रं च त्रिविधं कर्मणः फलम् ।
भवत्यत्यागिनां प्रेत्य न तु संन्यासिनां क्वचित् ॥ १२

It is not right to give up actions which are obligatory; and if they are misunderstood and ignored, it is the result of sheer ignorance.

To avoid an action through fear of physical suffering, because it is likely to be painful, is to act from passion, and the benefit of renunciation will not follow.

He who performs an obligatory action, because he believes it to be a duty which ought to be done, without any personal desire either to do the act or to receive any return—such renunciation is Pure.

The wise man who has attained purity, whose doubts are solved, who is filled with the spirit of self-abnegation, does not shrink from action because it brings pain, nor does he desire it because it brings pleasure.

But since those still in the body cannot entirely avoid action, in their case abandonment of the fruit of action is considered as complete renunciation.

For those who cannot renounce all desire, the fruit of action hereafter is threefold—good, evil, and partly good and partly evil. But for him who has renounced, there is none.

I will tell thee now, O Mighty Man, the five causes which, according to the final decision of philosophy, must concur before an action can be accomplished.

They are a body, a personality, physical organs, their manifold activity and destiny.

Whatever action a man perform, whether by muscular effort or by speech or by thought, and whether it be right or wrong, these five are the essential causes.

But the fool who supposes, because of his immature judgement, that it is his own Self alone that acts, he perverts the truth and does not see rightly.

He who has no pride, and whose intellect is unalloyed by attachment, even though he kill these people, yet he does not kill them, and his act does not bind him.

Knowledge, the knower and the object of knowledge, these are the threefold incentives to action; and the act, the actor and the instrument are the threefold constituents.

The knowledge, the act and the doer differ according to the Qualities. Listen to this too:

That knowledge which sees the One Indestructible in all beings, the One Indivisible in all separate lives, may be truly called Pure Knowledge.

The knowledge which thinks of the manifold existence in all beings as separate — that comes from Passion.

But that which clings blindly to one idea as if it were all, without logic, truth or insight, that has its origin in Darkness.

पञ्चैतानि महाबाहो कारणानि निबोध मे ।
सांख्ये कृतान्ते प्रोक्तानि सिद्धये सर्वकर्मणाम् ॥ १३

अधिष्ठानं तथा कर्ता करणं च पृथग्विधम् ।
विविधाश्च पृथक्चेष्टा दैवं चैवात्र पञ्चमम् ॥ १४

शरीरवाङ्मनोभिर्यत्कर्म प्रारभते नरः ।
न्याय्यं वा विपरीतं वा पञ्चैते तस्य हेतवः ॥ १५

तत्रैवं सति कर्तारमात्मानं केवलं तु यः ।
पश्यत्यकृतबुद्धित्वान्न स पश्यति दुर्मतिः ॥ १६

यस्य नाहंकृतो भावो बुद्धिर्यस्य न लिप्यते ।
हत्वापि स इमाँल्लोकान्न हन्ति न निबध्यते ॥ १७

ज्ञानं ज्ञेयं परिज्ञाता त्रिविधा कर्मचोदना ।
करणं कर्म कर्तेति त्रिविधः कर्मसंग्रहः ॥ १८

ज्ञानं कर्म च कर्ता च त्रिधैव गुणभेदतः ।
प्रोच्यते गुणसंख्याने यथावच्छृणु तान्यपि ॥ १९

सर्वभूतेषु येनैकं भावमव्ययमीक्षते ।
अविभक्तं विभक्तेषु तज्ज्ञानं विद्धि सात्त्विकम् ॥ २०

पृथक्त्वेन तु यज्ज्ञानं नानाभावान्पृथग्विधान् ।
वेत्ति सर्वेषु भूतेषु तज्ज्ञानं विद्धि राजसम् ॥ २१

यत्तु कृत्स्नवदेकस्मिन्कार्ये सक्तमहैतुकम् ।
अतत्त्वार्थवदल्पं च तत्तामसमुदाहृतम् ॥ २२

नियतं सङ्गरहितमरागद्वेषतः कृतम् ।
अफलप्रेप्सुना कर्म यत्तत्सात्त्विकमुच्यते ॥ २३
यत्तु कामेप्सुना कर्म साहंकारेण वा पुनः ।
क्रियते बहुलायासं तद्राजसमुदाहृतम् ॥ २४
अनुबन्धं क्षयं हिंसामनपेक्ष्य च पौरुषम् ।
मोहादारभ्यते कर्म यत्तत्तामसमुच्यते ॥ २५
मुक्तसङ्गोऽनहंवादी धृत्युत्साहसमन्वितः ।
सिद्ध्यसिद्ध्योर्निर्विकारः कर्ता सात्त्विक उच्यते ॥ २६
रागी कर्मफलप्रेप्सुर्लुब्धो हिंसात्मकोऽशुचिः ।
हर्षशोकान्वितः कर्ता राजसः परिकीर्तितः ॥ २७
अयुक्तः प्राकृतः स्तब्धः शठो नैष्कृतिकोऽलसः ।
विषादी दीर्घसूत्री च कर्ता तामस उच्यते ॥ २८

An obligatory action done by one who is disinterested, who neither likes it nor dislikes it, and gives no thought to the consequences that follow, such an action is Pure.

But even though an action involve the most strenuous endeavour, yet if the doer is seeking to gratify his desires, and is filled with personal vanity, it may be assumed to originate in Passion.

An action undertaken through delusion, and with no regard to the spiritual issues involved, or to the real capacity of the doer, or to the injury which may follow, such an act may be assumed to be the product of Ignorance.

But when a man has no sentiment and no personal vanity, when he possesses courage and confidence, cares not whether he succeeds or fails, then his action arises from Purity.

In him who is impulsive, greedy, looking for reward, violent, impure, torn between joy and sorrow, it may be assumed that in him Passion is predominant.

While he whose purpose is infirm, who is low-minded, stubborn, dishonest, malicious, indolent, despondent, pro-crastinating—he may be assumed to be in Darkness.

बुद्धेर्भेदं धृतेश्चैव गुणतस्त्रिविधं शृणु ।
प्रोच्यमानमशेषेण पृथक्त्वेन धनंजय ॥ २९
प्रवृत्तिं च निवृत्तिं च कार्याकार्ये भयाभये ।
बन्धं मोक्षं च या वेत्ति बुद्धिः सा पार्थ सात्त्विकी ॥ ३०
यया धर्ममधर्मं च कार्यं चाकार्यमेव च ।
अयथावत्प्रजानाति बुद्धिः सा पार्थ राजसी ॥ ३१
अधर्मं धर्ममिति या मन्यते तमसावृता ।
सर्वार्थान्विपरीतांश्च बुद्धिः सा पार्थ तामसी ॥ ३२
धृत्या यया धारयते मनःप्राणेन्द्रियक्रियाः ।
योगेनाव्यभिचारिण्या धृतिः सा पार्थ सात्त्विकी ॥ ३३
यया तु धर्मकामार्थान्धृत्या धारयतेऽर्जुन ।
प्रसङ्गेन फलाकाङ्क्षी धृतिः सा पार्थ राजसी ॥ ३४
यया स्वप्नं भयं शोकं विषादं मदमेव च ।
न विमुञ्चति दुर्मेधा धृतिः सा पार्थ तामसी ॥ ३५

Reason and conviction are threefold, according to the Quality which is dominant. I will explain them fully and severally, O Arjuna!

That intellect which understands the creation and dissolution of life, what actions should be done and what not, which discriminates between fear and fearlessness, bondage and deliverance, that is Pure.

The intellect which does not understand what is right and what is wrong, and what should be done and what not, is under the sway of Passion.

And that which, shrouded in Ignorance, thinks wrong right, and sees everything perversely, O Arjuna, that intellect is ruled by Darkness.

The conviction and steady concentration by which the mind, the vitality and the senses are controlled—O Arjuna! They are the product of Purity.

The conviction which always holds fast to rituals, to self-interest and wealth, for the sake of what they may bring forth—that comes from Passion.

And that which clings perversely to false idealism, fear, grief, despair and vanity is the product of Ignorance.

सुखं त्विदानीं त्रिविधं शृणु मे भरतर्षभ ।
अभ्यासाद्रमते यत्र दुःखान्तं च निगच्छति ॥ ३६
यत्तदग्रे विषमिव परिणामेऽमृतोपमम् ।
तत्सुखं सात्त्विकं प्रोक्तमात्मबुद्धिप्रसादजम् ॥ ३७
विषयेन्द्रियसंयोगाद्यत्तदग्रेऽमृतोपमम् ।
परिणामे विषमिव तत्सुखं राजसं स्मृतम् ॥ ३८
यदग्रे चानुबन्धे च सुखं मोहनमात्मनः ।
निद्रालस्यप्रमादोत्थं तत्तामसमुदाहृतम् ॥ ३९
न तदस्ति पृथिव्यां वा दिवि देवेषु वा पुनः ।
सत्त्वं प्रकृतिजैर्मुक्तं यदेभिः स्यात्त्रिभिर्गुणैः ॥ ४०

ब्राह्मणक्षत्रियविशां शूद्राणां च परंतप ।
कर्माणि प्रविभक्तानि स्वभावप्रभवैर्गुणैः ॥ ४१
शमो दमस्तपः शौचं क्षान्तिरार्जवमेव च ।
ज्ञानं विज्ञानमास्तिक्यं ब्रह्मकर्म स्वभावजम् ॥ ४२
शौर्यं तेजो धृतिर्दाक्ष्यं युद्धे चाप्यपलायनम् ।
दानमीश्वरभावश्च क्षत्रकर्म स्वभावजम् ॥ ४३
कृषिगोरक्ष्यवाणिज्यं वैश्यकर्म स्वभावजम् ।
परिचर्यात्मकं कर्म शूद्रस्यापि स्वभावजम् ॥ ४४
स्वे स्वे कर्मण्यभिरतः संसिद्धिं लभते नरः ।
स्वकर्मनिरतः सिद्धिं यथा विन्दति तच्छृणु ॥ ४५

Hear further the three kinds of pleasure. That which increases day after day and delivers one from misery,

Which at first seems like poison but afterwards acts like nectar—that pleasure is Pure, for it is born of Wisdom.

That which at first is like nectar, because the senses revel in their objects, but in the end acts like poison—that pleasure arises from Passion.

While the pleasure which from first to last merely drugs the senses, which springs from indolence, lethargy and folly—that pleasure flows from Ignorance.

There is nothing anywhere on earth or in the higher worlds which is free from the three Qualities—for they are born of Nature.

O Arjuna! The duties of the spiritual teachers, the soldiers, the traders and the servants have all been fixed according to the dominant Quality in their nature.

Serenity, self-restraint, austerity, purity, forgiveness, as well as uprightness, knowledge, wisdom and faith in God—these constitute the duty of a spiritual Teacher.

Valour, glory, firmness, skill, generosity, steadiness in battle and ability to rule—these constitute the duty of a soldier. They flow from his own nature.

Agriculture, protection of the cow and trade are the duty of a trader, again in accordance with his nature. The duty of a servant is to serve, and that too agrees with his nature.

Perfection is attained when each attends diligently to his duty. Listen and I will tell you how it is attained by him who always minds his own duty.

Man reaches perfection by dedicating his actions to God,
Who is the source of all being, and fills everything.

It is better to do one's own duty, however defective it may
be, than to follow the duty of another, however well one
may perform it. He who does his duty as his own nature
reveals it, never sins.

The duty that of itself falls to one's lot should not be abandoned, though it may have its defects. All acts are marred by
defects, as fire is obscured by smoke.

He whose mind is entirely detached, who has conquered
himself, whose desires have vanished, by his renunciation
reaches that stage of perfect freedom where action completes
itself and leaves no seed.

I will now state briefly how he, who has reached perfection,
finds the Eternal Spirit, the state of Supreme Wisdom.

Guided always by pure reason, bravely restraining himself,
renouncing the objects of sense and giving up attachment
and hatred;

Enjoying solitude, abstemious, his body, mind and speech
under perfect control, absorbed in meditation, he becomes
free — always filled with the spirit of renunciation.

Having abandoned selfishness, power, arrogance, anger and
desire, possessing nothing of his own and having attained
peace, he is fit to join the Eternal Spirit.

And when he becomes one with the Eternal, and his soul
knows the bliss that belongs to the Self, he feels no desire and
no regret, he regards all beings equally and enjoys the blessing of supreme devotion to Me.

By such devotion, he sees Me, who I am and what I am; and
thus realising the Truth, he enters My Kingdom.

Relying on Me in all his actions and doing them for My
sake, he attains, by My Grace, Eternal and Unchangeable
Life.

यतः प्रवृत्तिर्भूतानां येन सर्वमिदं ततम् ।
स्वकर्मणा तमभ्यर्च्य सिद्धिं विन्दति मानवः ॥ ४६

श्रेयान्स्वधर्मो विगुणः परधर्मात्स्वनुष्ठितात् ।
स्वभावनियतं कर्म कुर्वन्नाप्नोति किल्बिषम् ॥ ४७

सहजं कर्म कौन्तेय सदोषमपि न त्यजेत् ।
सर्वारम्भा हि दोषेण धूमेनाग्निरिवावृताः ॥ ४८

असक्तबुद्धिः सर्वत्र जितात्मा विगतस्पृहः ।
नैष्कर्म्यसिद्धिं परमां संन्यासेनाधिगच्छति ॥ ४९

सिद्धिं प्राप्तो यथा ब्रह्म तथाप्नोति निबोध मे ।
समासेनैव कौन्तेय निष्ठा ज्ञानस्य या परा ॥ ५०

बुद्ध्या विशुद्धया युक्तो धृत्यात्मानं नियम्य च ।
शब्दादीन्विषयांस्त्यक्त्वा रागद्वेषौ व्युदस्य च ॥ ५१

विविक्तसेवी लघ्वाशी यतवाक्कायमानसः ।
ध्यानयोगपरो नित्यं वैराग्यं समुपाश्रितः ॥ ५२

अहंकारं बलं दर्पं कामं क्रोधं परिग्रहम् ।
विमुच्य निर्ममः शान्तो ब्रह्मभूयाय कल्पते ॥ ५३

ब्रह्मभूतः प्रसन्नात्मा न शोचति न काङ्क्षति ।
समः सर्वेषु भूतेषु मद्भक्तिं लभते पराम् ॥ ५४

भक्त्या मामभिजानाति यावान्यश्चास्मि तत्त्वतः ।
ततो मां तत्त्वतो ज्ञात्वा विशते तदनन्तरम् ॥ ५५

सर्वकर्माण्यपि सदा कुर्वाणो मद्व्यपाश्रयः ।
मत्प्रसादादवाप्नोति शाश्वतं पदमव्ययम् ॥ ५६

Surrender then thy actions unto Me, live in Me, concentrate thine intellect on Me, and think always of Me.

Fix but thy mind on Me, and by My grace thou shalt overcome the obstacles in thy path. But if, misled by pride, thou wilt not listen, then indeed thou shalt be lost.

If thou in thy vanity thinkest of avoiding this fight, thy will shall not be fulfilled, for Nature herself will compel thee.

O Arjuna! Thy duty binds thee. From thine own nature has it arisen, and that which in thy delusion thou desirest not to do, that very thing thou shalt do. Thou art helpless.

God dwells in the hearts of all beings, O Arjuna! He causes them to revolve as it were on a wheel by His mystic power.

With all thy strength, fly unto Him and surrender thyself, and by His grace shalt thou attain Supreme Peace and reach the Eternal Home.

Thus have I revealed to thee the Truth, the Mystery of mysteries. Having thought it over, thou art free to act as thou wilt.

चेतसा सर्वकर्माणि मयि संन्यस्य मत्परः ।
बुद्धियोगमुपाश्रित्य मच्चित्तः सततं भव ॥ ५७
मच्चित्तः सर्वदुर्गाणि मत्प्रसादात्तरिष्यसि ।
अथ चेत्त्वमहंकाराब्ब श्रोष्यसि विनङ्क्ष्यसि ॥ ५८
यदहंकारमाश्रित्य न योत्स्य इति मन्यसे ।
मिथ्यैष व्यवसायस्ते प्रकृतिस्त्वां नियोक्ष्यति ॥ ५९
स्वभावजेन कौन्तेय निबद्धः स्वेन कर्मणा ।
कर्तुं नेच्छसि यन्मोहात्करिष्यस्यवशोऽपि तत् ॥ ६०
ईश्वरः सर्वभूतानां हृद्देशेऽर्जुन तिष्ठति ।
भ्रामयन्सर्वभूतानि यन्त्रारूढानि मायया ॥ ६१
तमेव शरणं गच्छ सर्वभावेन भारत ।
तत्प्रसादात्परां शान्तिं स्थानं प्राप्स्यसि शाश्वतम् ॥ ६२
इति ते ज्ञानमाख्यातं गुह्याद्गुह्यतरं मया ।
विमृश्यैतदशेषेण यथेच्छसि तथा कुरु ॥ ६३

Only listen once more to My last word, the deepest secret of all; thou art My beloved, thou art My friend, and I speak for thy welfare.

Dedicate thyself to Me, worship Me, sacrifice all for Me, prostrate thyself before Me, and to Me thou shalt surely come. Truly do I pledge thee; thou art My own beloved.

Give up then thy earthly duties, surrender thyself to Me only. Do not be anxious; I will absolve thee from all thy sin.

Speak not this to one who has not practised austerities, or to him who does not love, or who will not listen, or who mocks.

But he who teaches this great secret to My devotees, his is the highest devotion, and verily he shall come unto Me.

Nor is there among men any who can perform a service dearer to Me than this, or any man on earth more beloved by Me than he.

He who will study this spiritual discourse of ours, I assure thee, he shall thereby worship Me at the altar of Wisdom.

Yea, he who listens to it with faith, and without doubt, even he, freed from evil, shall rise to the worlds which the virtuous attain through righteous deeds.

O Arjuna! Hast thou listened attentively to My words? Has thy ignorance and thy delusion gone?

Arjuna replied: My Lord! O Immutable One! My delusion has fled. By Thy Grace, O Changeless One, the light has dawned. My doubts are gone, and I stand before Thee ready to do Thy will."

सर्वगुह्यतमं भूयः शृणु मे परमं वचः ।
इष्टोऽसि मे दृढमिति ततो वक्ष्यामि ते हितम् ॥ ६४
मन्मना भव मद्भक्तो मद्याजी मां नमस्कुरु ।
मामेवैष्यसि सत्यं ते प्रतिजाने प्रियोऽसि मे ॥ ६५
सर्वधर्मान्परित्यज्य मामेकं शरणं व्रज ।
अहं त्वा सर्वपापेभ्यो मोक्षयिष्यामि मा शुचः ॥ ६६
इदं ते नातपस्काय नाभक्ताय कदाचन ।
न चाशुश्रूषवे वाच्यं न च मां योऽभ्यसूयति ॥ ६७
य इदं परमं गुह्यं मद्भक्तेष्वभिधास्यति ।
भक्तिं मयि परां कृत्वा मामेवैष्यत्यसंशयः ॥ ६८
न च तस्मान्मनुष्येषु कश्चिन्मे प्रियकृत्तमः ।
भविता न च मे तस्मादन्यः प्रियतरो भुवि ॥ ६९
अध्येष्यते च य इमं धर्म्यं संवादमावयोः ।
ज्ञानयज्ञेन तेनाहमिष्टः स्यामिति मे मतिः ॥ ७०
श्रद्धावाननसूयश्च शृणुयादपि यो नरः ।
सोऽपि मुक्तः शुभाँल्लोकान्प्राप्नुयात्पुण्यकर्मणाम् ॥७१
कच्चिदेतच्छ्रुतं पार्थ त्वयैकाग्रेण चेतसा ।
कच्चिदज्ञानसंमोहः प्रनष्टस्ते धनंजय ॥ ७२
    अर्जुन उवाच ।
नष्टो मोहः स्मृतिर्लब्धा त्वत्प्रसादान्मयाच्युत ।
स्थितोऽस्मि गतसंदेहः करिष्ये वचनं तव ॥ ७३

Sanjaya told: "Thus have I heard this rare, wonderful and soul-stirring discourse of the Lord Shri Krishna and the great-souled Arjuna.

Through the blessing of the sage Vyasa, I listened to this secret and noble science from the lips of its Master, the Lord Shri Krishna.

O King! The more I think of that marvellous and holy discourse, the more I lose myself in joy.

As memory recalls again and again the exceeding beauty of the Lord, I am filled with amazement and happiness.

Wherever is the Lord Shri Krishna, the Prince of Wisdom, and wherever is Arjuna, the Great Archer, I am more than convinced that good fortune, victory, happiness and righteousness will follow."

Thus, in the Holy Book the Bhagavad Gita, one of the Upanishads, in the Science of the Supreme Spirit, in the Art of Self-Knowledge, in the colloquy between the Divine Lord Shri Krishna and the Prince Arjuna, stands the eighteenth chapter, entitled: The Spirit of Renunciation.

May the Lord Shri Krishna bless you!

संजय उवाच ।
इत्यहं वासुदेवस्य पार्थस्य च महात्मनः ।
संवादमिममश्रौषमद्भुतं रोमहर्षणम् ॥ ७४
व्यासप्रसादाच्छ्रुतवानेतद्गुह्ममहं परम् ।
योगं योगेश्वरात्कृष्णात्साक्षात्कथयतः स्वयम् ॥ ७५
राजन्संस्मृत्य संस्मृत्य संवादमिममद्भुतम् ।
केशवार्जुनयोः पुण्यं हृष्यामि च मुहुर्मुहुः ॥ ७६
तच्च संस्मृत्य संस्मृत्य रूपमत्यद्भुतं हरेः ।
विस्मयो मे महान्राजन्हृष्यामि च पुनः पुनः ॥ ७७
यत्र योगेश्वरः कृष्णो यत्र पार्थो धनुर्धरः ।
तत्र श्रीर्विजयो भूतिर्ध्रुवा नीतिर्मतिर्मम ॥ ७८

इति श्रीमद्भगवद्गीतासु अष्टादशोऽध्यायः ॥ १८ ॥

श्रीमद्भगवद्गीता समाप्ता ॥

Gwyneth Foden

A NOTE ABOUT THE TRANSLATOR

Shri Purohit Swami was born into a religious and wealthy family in Badnera, India, in 1882. He studied philosophy and law, received his LL.B. from Deccan College, Poona, married and had three children. However, he did not practice law, and instead spent his entire life in spiritual devotion. He wrote in his native Marathi, in Hindi, Sanskrit and English—poems, songs, a play, a novel, a commentary on *The Bhagavad Gita* and an autobiography. He left India in 1930 at the suggestion of his Master to interpret the religious life of India for the West, and made his new home in England. It was here that he produced beautiful translations of *The Bhagavad Gita*, Patanjali's *Aphorisms of Yoga* and—in collaboration with his great friend, the Irish poet W. B. Yeats—*The Ten Principal Upanishads*. He died in 1946.

A NOTE ABOUT THE PHOTOGRAPHS

The photographs in this book were taken on location in India, Nepal, Sikkim, Java and Bali. The photographic equipment used was made by Leica, Nikon, Rolleiflex and Hasselblad. The negatives are on Kodak film, and the photographs were originally printed on Agfa paper.

On location, in areas of the world that frequently present difficulties for the traveller, I had the good fortune to be helped generously by many people who are living proof of Krishna's statement that "spirituality is the art of living." I want to express my deepest thanks to: Monica Suder and Cliff Coulston; Tjakorda G'de Parta; Made Djimat, Master of Dancing; Murni and Pat Scanlan; Tjakorda Oka Harsana; Mr. and Mrs. Ida Bagus Bajra; Ian Caldwell; Ketut Madra; Dewa Ketut Baru; Dewa Made Mudita; Linda Lieberman; Ellen McNeilly; Ann Close; Curtis B. Bruce; Karen Goodman; Wayne Lockwood; Ida Bagus Gelodog and family; His Holiness the Fourteenth Gyalwa Karmapa; His Holiness Kalu, Rinpoche; His Holiness Khamtul, Rinpoche; Atul and Lolly Vedya; Danielle and Andrew Toth; Joe Helfin; Susan and Cody Schwaiko; Philip Makenna; Fred Papel; Lionel Craven; Robert Hillman; Cal Mullin; Roger and Betty Baird; Beverly Caroline Labine; Jan and Ed Hauben; Tamara Wasserman; Ellen Elisofon; George Hoffberg; Barry Silberstang; Ellen and Jim Tyack; Crescenzo Giasullo.

Last, I'd like to thank three people without whose help, trust and confidence this work would have been impossible: my editor, Toinette Lippe; my agent, Susan Ann Protter; and Arky Robbins, who helped in more ways than I can say here.

The photographs are dedicated to Mary Letterii.

C.B.

Arky Robbins

A NOTE ABOUT THE PHOTOGRAPHER

Born in 1946, Curt Bruce is an American photographer whose camera has taken him on extended field trips to North Africa, Europe, Greece, the Caribbean, India, Nepal and Indonesia. After studying painting at the Cooper Union in New York City, he moved to San Francisco. His pictures have appeared in *Natural History*, *Smithsonian*, *Architectural Forum*, *Artforum*, *Rolling Stone* and *California Living*. His work has been exhibited throughout the United States, and he is the photographer of *The Great Houses of San Francisco* (Knopf, 1974), *Revelations of New England Architecture* (Viking/Grossman, 1975), and the author and photographer of *The Great Houses of New Orleans* (Knopf, 1977). He is currently at work on his first film.

A NOTE ON THE TYPE

The text of this book was set in a film version of Bembo, the well-known monotype face. The original cutting of Bembo was made by Francesco Griffo of Bologna only a few years after Columbus discovered America. It was named for Pietro Bembo, the celebrated Renaissance writer and humanist scholar who was made a cardinal and served as secretary to Pope Leo X.

Sturdy, well-balanced and finely proportioned, Bembo is a face of rare beauty. It is, at the same time, extremely legible in all of its sizes.

Composed by Superior Printing, Champaign, Illinois.

Printed and bound by Halliday Lithographers, West Hanover, Massachusetts.

Designed by Clint Anglin.